BOA
EDITIONS
LIMITED

BODY LANGUAGE

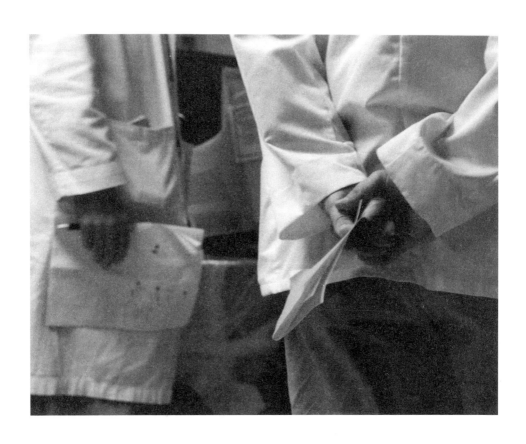

BODY LANGUAGE

POEMS OF THE MEDICAL TRAINING EXPERIENCE

Edited by

Neeta Jain
Dagan Coppock
Stephanie Brown Clark

BOA ANTHOLOGY SERIES, NO. 2

BOA EDITIONS, LTD. ❋ ROCHESTER, NY ❋ 2006

First Edition
06 07 08 09 7 6 5 4 3 2 1

Publications by BOA Editions, Ltd.—a not-for-profit corporation under section 501 (c) (3) of
the United States Internal Revenue Code—are made possible with the assistance of grants from
the Literature Program of the New York State Council on the Arts; the Literature Program
of the National Endowment for the Arts; the County of Monroe, NY; the Lannan Foundation
for support of the Lannan Translations Selection Series; the Sonia Raiziss Giop Charitable
Foundation; the Mary S. Mulligan Charitable Trust; the Rochester Area Community Founda-
tion; the Arts & Cultural Council for Greater Rochester; the Steeple-Jack Fund; the Elizabeth
F. Cheney Foundation; the Chesonis Family Foundation; the Ames-Amzalak Memorial Trust
in memory of Henry Ames, Semon Amzalak and Dan Amzalak; the Witter Bynner Founda-
tion for Poetry; and contributions from many individuals nationwide.

Cover Design: Lisa Mauro
Cover Art: Ken Kao
Photographs: Ken Kao
Interior Design and Composition: Richard Foerster
Manufacturing: McNaughton & Gunn, Lithographers
BOA Logo: Mirko

Library of Congress Cataloging-in-Publication Data

Body language : poems of the medical training experience / edited by Neeta
Jain, Dagan Coppock, and Stephanie Brown Clark.— 1st ed.
     p. cm. — (BOA anthology series ; no.2)
     ISBN 1–929918–86–0 (pbk. : alk. paper)
1. Medicine—Study and teaching—Poetry. 2. Physicians—Poetry. 3.
American poetry—21st century. I. Jain, Neeta. II. Coppock, Dagan. III.
Clark, Stephanie Brown, 1958– IV. Title. V. Series.

PS595.M43B63 2006
821.008'03561—dc22

2006007142

NATIONAL
ENDOWMENT
FOR THE ARTS

BOA Editions, Ltd.
Thom Ward, Editor
David Oliveiri, Co-Chair
Glenn William, Co-Chair
A. Poulin, Jr., President & Founder (1938–1996)
260 East Avenue, Rochester, NY 14604
www.boaeditions.org

State of the Arts
NYSCA

To all students of medicine

Contents

※   *Intern*

Resident

Attending

Introduction

As part of our medical school orientation program at Stony Brook, I recently met with a small group of new students. To stimulate discussion, I presented a short video clip from a television program that depicts "real life" events at a trauma center. In this segment a resident walked into a waiting room and spoke to the family of a nine-year-old boy who had just been run over by a truck. The boy was brain dead. This was the resident's first experience at giving bad news.

The video was gripping. Even though we were strangers to one another, the students had little difficulty expressing their heartfelt anxieties and beliefs. Some admired the resident because she came across as steady and cool. She told the family the boy was dead, but showed no sign of emotion. Other students criticized her performance, saying that she lacked heart. They believed the doctor should have displayed her own sorrow at the boy's death. The group was divided between those who said the doctor ought to be a pillar of strength and those who wanted her to be more interactive and emotional. In their minds strength and emotion are mutually exclusive.

These opposing points of view made for a productive discussion. Interestingly, I noticed that individual students struggled internally with the issue, since most recognized the importance of steadiness *and* of tenderness in clinical encounters. For some of them, this may have been the first time they had to confront (even if only vicariously) the tension between detachment and connection, objectivity and subjectivity, steadiness and tenderness that lies at the heart of medical practice. How can a physician open herself up and become a compassionate presence for the patient, while at the same time maintaining sufficient detachment to think clearly and make objective decisions?

Although dominant in medicine today, the belief that emotional response weakens us is by no means evidence-based. In her essay "Metaphor and Memory," Cynthia Ozick observed that physicians cultivate detachment from their patients because they are afraid of finding themselves "too frail . . . to enter into psychological twinship with the even frailer souls of the sick." In other words, Ozick believes that detachment is a sign of weakness, rather than strength.

The tension between steadiness and tenderness in medicine can generate enormous creative energy. This is particularly true nowadays when we rely so much on machines and techniques, which require so much of our attention that we have little time to let in the patient-as-person. Those who are sensitive to this tension need to find coping mechanisms to find their own resolution. For those so inclined, creative writing, especially poetry, offers a way of giving voice to the joy and pain of medical practice. Thus, it is no wonder that our age of technical, depersonalized medicine has also—and perhaps somewhat unexpectedly—seen a spectacular flowering of poetry written by physicians.

Physician-poets are popping up all over. Major medical journals publish their work. Their poems are taught in medical school. Poetry readings appear on the programs of national medical meetings. And the deep connections between medicine, poetry, and healing are openly discussed. Of course, the downside is that there are probably more medical poets than there are readers of poetry, as is also true among the general public. Nonetheless, poetry in medicine is making its voice heard.

In *Body Language*, the editors have chosen poems that evoke the entire spectrum of medical education, beginning with medical school and residency training, and ending with full medical citizenship, as an attending physician. The fine poetry in this collection speaks to the sensitivity and experience of a talented group of student and practicing physicians. The book's medical education framework provides the reader with an in-depth history of the conflict (and ultimately dynamic tension) between tenderness and steadiness in medical practice. As Katherine Freeman writes in "Picture This,"

> Yet I keep standing, searching, for that one structure
> that will make this body complete, that will make my self
> feel found . . .

Likewise, Michael Jacobs ("Falling Through") cries out, "I want to taste my life / Before it melts away." Yet, the work must be done. As a clinical student, Kelley Jean White reacts to telling her patient that he will die from cancer of the pancreas ("Pandora"):

> Leaving his room, crying,
> avoiding classmates,
> I take the back stairs.
> I find myself locked,
> coatless, in the courtyard outside.

In "Internship in Seattle" by Emily R. Transue, the young doctor confesses, "When I first came here I got wet a lot." But then she acquires the raincoat of medical objectivity, "Then just recently / I got myself a raincoat; / It's made of shiny clear plastic . . . Nothing can get through." Despite the medical milieu though, these poets, at least, have survived with their sensitivity intact, and, perhaps, even deepened:

> between the endless rounds
> the endless dyings
>
> still beats
> a poet's heart
>
> and it pounds again
> and pounds again   *(Jerald Winakur, "Auscultation")*

Don't get me wrong. These poems are definitely not all variations on a serious theme. You'll find irony, humor, love, and joy here, too. You'll find the enormous energy of youth and the retrospection of age. You'll find it all.

—Jack Coulehan

Medical Student, First Year

※ *Meghann Kaiser*

Where I Left Off

Inspiration is
Taking up where I left off.

Rosario is a place for new mornings.
Or at least new to me.
I can't remember the last time I was up before sunrise.
But here, the cool is almost acidic, the dew dense,
The ocean water skitters
Over a dimpled shore two blocks past,
And I am lying on the rooftop of an abandoned shoe factory,
Exposed,
At last.

I'm going to be a poet.
I'm going to workshops,
Learn to express my precise persona,
In haikus about white lilies.
I'll major in literature, applied alliteration
And well-wired metaphors.
Words strung on fish line, puppets to the poet,
Will tip-toe, quiver along the circumference of
The unexpected.

No, I'm going to be a doctor.
I'm living in Irvine
With specimens of humanity strewn on stainless steel.
Trivia and textbooks.
Here, the climate is pre-programmed on my thermostat,
The hour I rise determined by panic.
The ocean is five miles away; I have not once visited it.
And sunrise through Venetian blinds
Tells me I'll be late for class.
I will recreate my art form in the image of myself.
A blood-rich tide I carry with me still,

Too scarlet for seas.
The rhythm I can't escape,
Neither in Rosario
Nor in Irvine.
It is me, but not mine made.

Take up your scalpel,
And write.

Happenstance

In Jersey City once
I happened to sleep
under the sign of Saint Margaret.
It was in a convent.
The nuns there had taken
a vow of silence.
Every room had its own sink.
Every sink had a crucifix
instead of a mirror.
They were down to eight nuns.
As it happened they let
Dartmouth boys
use the vacant cells.
Security, I suppose.
One of the boys let me in.
I had a manuscript in a box,
the required autobiographical
novel-in-progress.
I intended to show it to agents
in New York.
A hurricane happened.
The literary offices were closed.
The agents had all gone home
to Long Island.
I went to medical school.
I still have the box.
I don't know what happened
to the nuns.

Smoke, Going

I.

I watch my grandfather
as he drags through the penned waves
of a university pool, swimming

no doubt for the last time. Proud,
wrinkled legs stray and splay
like a child's under monkey bars,

but amidst the thrashings,
a central line holds: the fin
of his tumored spine

just beneath the surface. Stiff
as he is, the turns roll,
unfold in a perpendicular

corking off the wall that rights him
like a mother's even hand on her
lap-dozing toddler in church.

II.

Needle and plunge, daily now,
invade and crowd him
even more than this hospital

room already did. Move over.
I sit on my hands
to shut them up.

III.

Browned dusk: takeoff, and I
climb back into the haze. Leaving
all this brittle behind, once more,

for home, I cannot help
but thank the clouds that close
around this plane, angry

tufts of whispered candy. Dust
trapped by water. Water
made solid by dust.

Still Life in Number Seven

A prelude of iodine, a quickening,
a slipping away of friction,
then a slice that seemed to precede
its own motion of graceful opening

into a smoke-jellied scene
of avocado and pomegranate.
An abdomen, quartered
off with baby blue sheets,

unfolded beneath an unassuming
blade in my father's double-gloved hands
to reveal, for the first time,
the dirtied secrets of inner slick and color,

a crudeness I knew I could not
ask anyone to explain, a sight I felt sure
belonged back in its drawer.
But perhaps that is why our breathing,

even when it slides along without the help
of the gentle marking hand of a machine,
is so measured. So patiently insistent.
To give us time to sort through

the shifting nervousness
of organs packed neatly away.
To let us see the most ordinary and sterling
face of things. Color, texture,

light. Like a table forever set
for two. A wine bottle forlorn
and cold. A bowl of pears
that no one will ever eat.

Dagan Coppock

The Shaman's Apprentice

Ibadan, Nigeria

In the clearing of oil palms, I am offered the blade. From the shaman
I take the sweat-shellacked handle. Rust and dried blood pockmark
its surface. He draws the goat forward, leans to its ear, E se. *Thank you.*

His sons encircle the animal. Babatunde, Ositola flip its body, pin its legs.
Olufemi cranks his fingers beneath its jaw, pulls back the head. A flutter
of muscle, the goat's neck tenses. The shaman permits me—a
                    whisper, Cut.

Beads of sweat roll over my lips, my cheeks. Across my face, the shaman
wipes his hand, slings the sweat. On my skin I taste the oil, the salts
of his hands. Cut, he insists, till I draw the blade across the goat's neck.

The skin is tough, the blade is dull. I hack, strain at the cords of its throat.
The goat shakes. A wheeze of air, a gurgle of fluid escapes from my gash.
The shaman bends down to capture its blood in a bowl of brown clay.

All the way off, from his oldest, Olufemi. I chop my way through,
sever the head. Olufemi places it before the shrine of Ifa. From a
                    yellowed
Fanta bottle, the shaman gulps gin, wallows it in his mouth.

Through pursed lips, he sprays my head—a mist of the liquor,
                    saliva—then spits
the rest into the clay bowl of blood. With a knife, Olufemi removes
                    the goat's ears.
The shaman dips the ear into a gourd of red pepper, red palm oil. He
                    bathes the ear

in the clay bowl of blood. With the ear, he paints the twelve corners
                    of the Earth,
the cowries on my head. The blood sinks down, soaks the soil of my
                    scalp.

The shaman tells me, Asiri abo. *May your secrets be covered.*

I am turned from the shrine. The shaman is mumbling—low,
        hypnotic. The youngest sons—
Babatunde, Ositola—take my arms, lead me from Ifa. To my ears
        they speak,
just as their father, *From this day on, you cannot look behind you.*

Picture This

picture this:

Two A.M., Thursday night, I'm trying to find myself
amidst a brachial plexus of fibers; my nerves
shredded from picking at a torn-up stylopharyngeus, muscles
aching from overarching my secondary curvature, back
stiff as the epiglottis pierced with my blunt scalpel.

Yet I keep standing, searching, for that one structure
that will make this body complete, that will make my self
feel found in this body that I now feel is my own
as complex and torn up.

Anatomy Brain Wash

I take the Port Jefferson ferry to Connecticut
after my first anatomy exam;
out the window at Long Island Sound
a toddler struggles across the platform;
I note his spinal cord ends
at the third lumbar vertebra
(and not between one and two).

I drive off the ferry and take Interstate 95
to Route 91 across Highway 84 to the Mass Turnpike;
I travel a similar path from the descending aorta
to the celiac artery down the common hepatic
to the gastroduodenal.

At Cambridge, I down a few beers
and think of alcohol dehydrogenase,
fatty changes in my liver,
if glycogen synthesis is being inhibited;
a former roommate offers a cigarette
I decline thinking of pocked lung.

In a drunken stupor I hear the bartender yell last call.
I glance at the clock on the wall near the entrance;
Skene's glands are located at five and seven.

The next morning I am back at Starbucks,
too tired to eat; I order an espresso and
open my Netter's.

Anatomy Lab

She was stretched out naked,
young and blond,
wild and frightening

when the others were so old,
everyone at the steel table
pretending not to notice

the fortune of her body.
That first day I sliced off her breast,
scalpel circling round and round

the way I might halve a peach,
to study her glistening secrets
with detachment and awe.

We explored the deep insertions
where muscle joins bone,
subtracted her face, her arms,

plucked ovaries and heart like thieves,
but lost count of the treasures
severed from ourselves.

By year's end, brittle as guilt,
we hovered over our hollow creation,
pretending to look away

from the short blond braid
at the base of her skull
no one had the courage to cut.

Exposed (to her cadaver)

My fingers course
Through rivers of blood
Parched from seasons without rain
A man once despaired
To hold you so close
Yet never could see what I've seen
I must apologize
For not being gentle
This heartstring of yours
Must snap in the name of our intimacy
And your lovable idiosyncrasies
I call anomaly
As per the instructions
I commit you
To bits of fleeting recollection
And my gratitude
May only show when I too am discarded
To lie with decades exposed
A gift preserved in petals
Of desiccated rose

Apparition

I thought I saw him in the mall yesterday,

sitting on a bench wearing
thick glasses and a blue knit
hat from underneath which

peeked unkempt gray hair that
fell over his ears and framed his
vacant gaze. As I was walking

quickly by, I thought I saw my cadaver
sitting in the mall yesterday,

even though at that point his legs
were spread so far apart that the
one leg had decided to

sever its longstanding relationship
with the other, and even though I
had installed a skylight for each

of his eyes directly through the
frontal bone, and even though his
removable breastplate uncovered

a bereft thoracic vault,
and even though I knew the
shape of the rugae in his

stomach better than I knew the
shape of the nose on his face, and
even though it was not him,

it could have been.

※ *Bryan Maxwell*

Twice a Day After Meals

Even happiness, she once told me,
is a kind of scar. She was
sixteen or maybe seventeen
at the time, cheek pressed
to the white of a toilet rim
but no dinner to lose,
upstairs in the only house
I'd ever been in with an elevator
in the bedroom. When she lifted
her head, she was lopsided—
an apostrophe—from the red
mark of the bowl's lingering
touch, only temporary. *A spoonful
of medicine makes the sugar
go down.* Go down, sugar.

hungry

for Abby and Amanda

1

three baby carrots
i failed my chemistry exam today
i do not deserve to eat

2

two scoops of mashed potatoes
i miss my mother
i need some gravy

3

cookies
i am lonely
i eat a bag of Oreos

4

one banana. sixty bites
i look in the mirror
i must work out for six hours tomorrow

5

one rice cake with a pat of peanut butter
i vomit my dinner
i do not deserve to live

6

two liters of Diet Pepsi
i have found every hidden bathroom on campus
but i still haven't found myself.

7

four pieces of extra sugar-free peppermint gum
i have fainted three times this semester
i hope no one has noticed

8

a pint of Cherry Garcia
i don't know what it means anymore
when i say i'm hungry

A Final Memo to Dr. Carlo Urbani

You must have sat there like an awkward
silence
hanging heavy in the air.

The Doctor will see you now.

You were silence with a message, the silence
that made sound stop,
turning it from noise into music.

You were a thicket of thistle and burr,
clutching fabric at arms length—you held me
there, uprooted and choked as

you spoke, jaw unmoving though words came out,
notes dangling in suspended hesitation,
the world awaiting your crescendo.

Your eyes were resigned to the fact that you would
never again be touched
or swallowed by the arms
of an unconquered lover
floating into your bedroom on a supple
August breeze, standing disrobed before you
at the foot of the bed. She leans over
and brushes against your cheek before lifting the
sheets and drowning herself in you.

You must have lain there in your hospital bed, swaddled in white
sheets reminiscent of your white laboratory coat
that now I wear, altered and weighing heavy on my shoulders.

When you rolled over at night, did you ever wonder if
you were leaving the world in capable hands?

Desktop Daydream

Xeroxed wisdom
Flips in slippery pages through paper-slit fingers
And quivers in the beam of a desk lamp
To hit these pupils
Before my lids slam shut the night
Angered by the insistence of the carbonated
And the carbon-copied paper
Resting threateningly on my notebook

Somewhere
A man falls in a densely packed restaurant
Clatter of plates reverberates to tell me
It is time
Yes, there is a doctor in the house
I lie / tensely beside him
His pulse a drizzle next to my own storming chest
Wrestle with remembered modes of
Resuscitation / vaguely studied information
Curious crowd gathers in loud gasps
Fingers clasped I pound my fist
To crack open memory / but why can't he
Breathe?

Back to reality
No doctor in this house
Just a lazy town mouse experimenting
Atop a fence of frustration
A first-year imitation with a vision
And a new desk lamp
That makes the carbon shine
Just dimmer than a daydream
He's back at the Xerox machine
Paying for knowledge with common cents
And one day he'll find his place

With a tall white coat to hide the tail
It's all the rage / but till then
Stop the dream / open your eyes / take the copies
Turn the page.

Bruce's Prescription

Bruce Wayne knew
How to handle hurt
Pain ricocheting off plated chest
Dark cape cloaking the mess left
    From days in studious solitude
Driven by attitude and subtle rage
    Against the criminal plague
A uniform to mask fear
To reflect it in enemy eyes / a guise
So brittle it shattered every night
Little puzzle pieces scattered
    Across the cave
He battled loss
And knew the fight continued
A slave always knows his master
    By his laughter
But I bet Batman
Never took Tylenol
Never lay in bed asleep
Dissolving woes in soaked Kleenex
Invincibility refuted
    By yellowish sputum
Missing his rounds
To let a hanger wear his coat for the night
I bet Batman never ignored
Commissioner Gordon's call
Closed the drapes on the Gotham sky
    And let the signal pass him by
So as I lie here
Wrapped in toasty blankets
Buttered by morning sun
With a comic book to run my responsibilities away
I wonder if today I need to rise
Relieve the hanger of my guise and

Heed the call of my chosen career
Bruce Wayne would know what to do
But no one expects
A hero every day
. . . Do they?

※ *Bryan Maxwell*

Light from Dark

Just "LAUNDRY," that's all.
It seems right to him
that the sign says nothing else.
Some people go for a drive
in the country. Some reach
for the phone. Some smoke, run,
swim, eat. He comes here,
late at night, parks his silver Audi
behind the dumpster, tries to remember
not to use the *bleep-eep* button to lock.
He likes the tumble of angry socks
and the smells of the women: humidity,
hairspray, menthols. One of them sings
the jingle of the local Ford dealership
as she sorts a pillowcase, a green
towel, seven identical pairs
of navy blue work pants.
He doesn't speak, even when she stares
into the machines as if she might jump in
and spin clean, though he thinks
maybe he should. He can only admire
her hands as they fold, as they erase
the middle wrinkles of a bedsheet
by pulling, tight, on the edges.

Thursday

I stand alone.
My short, white coat trembles
from the pounding of my heart.
My big toe slides in and out of the hole
in my sock. It's soothing.

Raindrops creep down
my reflection in the window.
Familiar strangers surround me.
A young boy crawls around the floor
anxiously pushing a red fire engine.
His innocence shines the buttons on his overalls.

A businesswoman dressed in a suit
seems helpless with a blemish.
Two men sit together, a duet
occupying the same seats
side by side each week until split
by a brief hospital stay. A woman
called "Butch" finds her harbor
whispering music from a Walkman
placed gently upon her forehead.

I try not to stare at a young woman
eye blackened, face scratched,
hair tangled. Old men with scarred faces
cannot hear the laments of the young blind men
who cannot see their scars. Tall dancers sit taller
trying to maintain the dignity that made them,
at one time, so beautiful.
      Broadway is dying.

Each week, they sit. Gathered for a date
with a shiny needle, a plastic bag, and

twenty other risktakers. The room,
sterile, fresh, smells of pine and rubbing
alcohol. White specks in the carpet shine up
like stars. Serenity maintained by classical music
from two large speakers until a child crashes his hand
in a fishbowl of condoms. At least once a month
a rookie will mistake the bowl for a candy dish.

The institutional smell of this medical meadow
broken by the occasional passing of a figure
in white, swinging a stethoscope, stinking up
the air with the aroma of peppermints and coffee.
It smells like life.

Ducks

Winter and through the study carrels midnight screams
began to sound less comic; the first marriages fissioned,
others rocked—life rafts in need of some sight of land.

Pathology, physiology, the smell of death: vengeful
riders whipping me to learn one more bone.
Asleep I dreamed of textbooks with fading words.

Everywhere snow, a six-inch crust and frozen,
scentless air in Denver city park, my footsteps
broke the muffled day, brought mallards, widgeons,

Mexican ducks and ecstatic teals fighting for my crumbs—
I probably never learned the intricate tracery
of some lost nerve, traded for joyous greed.

Medical Student, Second Year

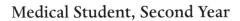

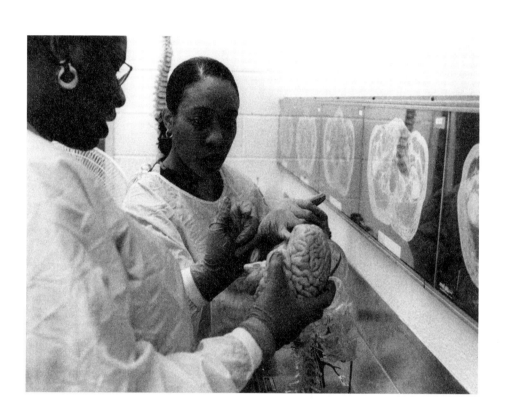

Richard M. Berlin

Medical School Lovers

One morning, while disease-slides flashed
and filled the lecture room with twilight blue,
the back door opened a sliver of light
and they entered holding hands.

A few of us turned, then the others,
four hundred eyes focused
on the couple at the door,
faces still flushed from making love,

their pleasure so certain.
The slides flashed on
and the lecturer persisted
but we were gone for the day,

still dazed by the way love can enter
our lives in a flash of light,
spinning our heads as we struggle
with lessons everyone learns in the dark.

C-Section

Afternoon pathology
lab, microscope immersion oil
late light through high tall windows above
the city. Melinda and I discovered
that we each wished to choose a name for our specimens.
I do not remember my choice, or hers, but our
instructor, a graying, handsome man of considerable
charm, named his "Dolores" and his much
much senior colleague, asked to confer over slides
of air-filled bowel wall, clicked a tongue in wonder,
"pneumatosis intestinalis—that must be Bill's gut,"
and we drank a toast, hot chocolate, to Bill, his
friend, fellow pathologist, husband, father, clarinetist,
gardener, one day scrubbing at the autopsy room sink,
then dead at eighty with total body failure, himself a specimen
for his peers. And you and I, then sweetly we thought
of dissecting each other, that I might at last one day
see what lay beneath the fine white parchment scar
childhood had left on your shin, your quick smooth
calves, your kneecap sliding, my sturdy stomach, tipped
uterus, thickened vocal cords, fragile butterfly thyroid
beneath a hollowed throat. . . . Not to happen.
My bones long ago forgot your skin touch. But you did
see the colossal purple cabbage of my womb cut
to release our breechling son, your hands tied the
knot at my appendix, while I saw only slick blood, felt
the odd push of air below the diaphragm, a heavy
tugging, hollow, pushing upward toward my heart.

Pathologic Vistas

A thin case of jiggling slides
Is opened near the microscope
To show glass plates set row on row,
Each one smudged with a bit of color,
Each one a particular person's end.

Fix the slide beneath the scope and see
An eosinophilic landscape
Swim up to you from its depths of minuteness.
Here is carcinoma of the breast;
See the cells swarm,
All a part of another world where cells have grown
Mutinous or failed in their duty.
But here's a white blood cell, patrolling the blood
Like some Roman centurion watching
The mist-shrouded, far bank of the Rhine
With civilization at his back
And the savagery of the unknown forest before him.

❋ *Joel J. Mathew*

Thoughts After First Visit to the Nursery

Break it to Becky gently:
the world is cold
and floats upon the mystery
of superficial hellos,
how-are-you's,
goodbyes.

When she cries,
cuddle her,
There, there,
                    hush, hush,
                              fret not—
by the time she knows,
her soft skull
will be calcified shut.

❊   *Richard M. Berlin*

Learning the Shapes

Five students
wear short white coats,
pockets bulging with note cards,
tuning forks, new stethoscopes.
Demanding consent
we snap on latex gloves,
smear index fingers with K-Y,
turn them over, spread them apart
and enter alone, one by one
to learn the shapes inside:
smooth chestnut, soft orange,
stone in a muddy field.
After wiping off the jelly
we wash our hands clean,
fingers sensitive
as a blind bluesman
who hears each note
an instant before
touching a tight steel string.

I Ask

A blood pressure check,
I put my hand on her wrist
to take a pulse,
a small, hard rectangle
protrudes from her skin
I ask. She says, A bullet.

I ask. She says, My husband shot me.
She is a small woman, quiet, calm.
Five times in the stomach. This bullet
somehow wayward, wandered to her wrist.

In the 50s, when I lived in Virginia, she says,
I had to have part of my stomach taken out.
They weren't sure if I'd live. But I did.

Michael Jacobs

Falling Through

It feels as though my life has slipped away,
Or I from it,
So suddenly and slowly.

I've been skating on black ice, out on a frozen ocean.
I have broken through, each drop piercing,
Each a single memory.
I don't want to see my life
Flash before my eyes.
I want to spread my soul out against the sun
So that my pain will melt away,

Leaving me my life to live.

I want to stay on the beach
And play in warm and shallow waters.
I want to dance the harmony of Mambo
Under the sun on Havana's Malecon.
I want to stand on the Great Wall of China
And wave to outer space
I want to explore the big white Alps
The way my tongue swirls about
This ice cream cone.

I want to taste my life
Before it melts away.

Pandora

September.
Second-year medical student.
An early patient interview
at the Massachusetts General Hospital.
Routine hernia repair planned, not done.
Abdomen opened and closed.
Filled with disease, cancer.

The patient is fifty-six,
a workingman, Irish.
I sit with him, notice
the St. Christopher medal
around his neck.
Can't hurt, can it? he laughs.
I have become his friend.

I bring him a coloring book picture
that shows this thing, this unfamiliar
organ that melted beneath our hands
at dissection:
Pancreas.

Leaving his room, crying,
avoiding classmates,
I take the back stairs.
I find myself locked,
coatless, in the courtyard outside.

Medical Student, Clinical Years

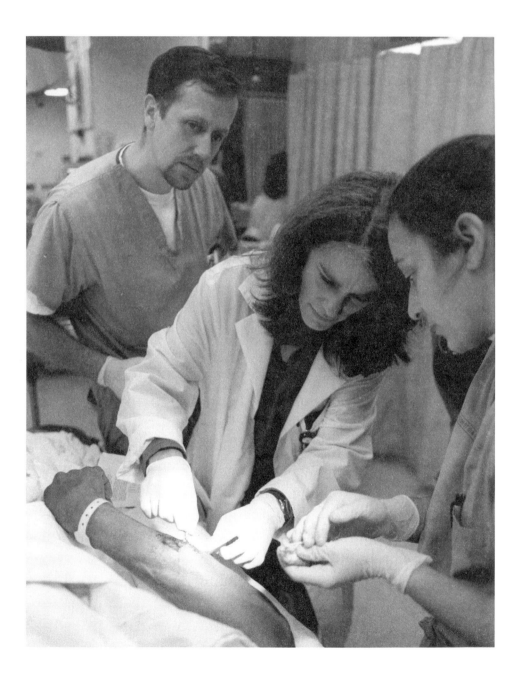

Brueghel at Bellevue

1.

The first two years were over. We exhaled,
And put aside our Physiology
And Histo books. We would no more be jailed
In lecture halls and labs. Biology
Would be different now, with humankind
Our texts. I couldn't wait to start, but feared
The endless hours of OB, the grind
Of surgery: I opted for the weird,
The wacky world of Doktors Jung and Freud;
I'd analyze my patients and explore
Their troubled minds, leave their spirits buoyed
Through the talk cure—and happiness restore.
Arriving prompt at 9:15 I knocked.
A buzzer let me in—the ward was locked.

2.

Neurotics and psychotics paced and chattered
To others, or themselves, or a sad clown
Who stared down from a poster, old and tattered.
The place was like the square in an old town
That Brueghel might have painted; so many things
Were happening at once—an old man growls,
A young man licks the floor, a woman sings
A mournful song about three lonely owls.
A tiny woman taps me on the waist,
I dreamed about the cockroaches last night,
I felt them—oh!—I am no longer chaste
And limps away as she bemoans her plight.
The guards stride by and snicker; it's no joke,
A patient gave a blow job for a smoke.

3.

Barefoot Mr. Diaz: Are you wearing
Panties? Blood rushed to my face: Why
Do you ask? Which was a little daring,
But it worked; he talked about the sky.
The resident said, Yes, that's what you say
When patients ask you questions about you.
Mr. Diaz loved to shock for play.
His specialty was subjects most taboo.
At group meetings, while others would complain
About the smokers, thieves, and river view,
From speaking to the group he would refrain
Preferring whispered comments to a few,
Or farting and then fainting for effect
While mumbling to his neighbor—I'm erect!

4.

She looked away and rolled her eyes and sighed;
I guess such words for her were nothing new.
I was disturbed at first, then tried to hide
A snort, which popped out, suddenly unglued.
I coughed to hide it, concentrated on
The meeting briefly, began to think about
The stories I could tell my friends, what fun!
The tale of Mr. Diaz, how he'd spout
Out things that simmered lewdly in his id,
Or loudly expel gas from either end.
But truth be told, I felt a little split—
My attempts to help him comprehend
Fell flat. Beneath the jokes, his manic glee,
I came to see: his world was closed to me.

5.

The gates slammed shut and we were ushered in
To a small room where sat a skinny man
Whose arms were scarred with tracks from heroin.
He gazed at us, then smiled, and began.
His name was Ricky, and he'd killed before,
But not this time. He'd tired of doing bills,
Then drove guns from state to state, a bore!
Then turned to hits. Now that had some more thrills,
And made the family proud, for he was good,
But then was caught and, terrified of jail,
He lit his arm on fire, as if wood;
A term in Bellevue did himself avail.
With a cop at his side would this young man refrain?
No—and that defines the criminally insane.

6.

Billy S. had lovely clear blue eyes,
A thatch of thick brown hair, and rotting teeth.
Psychotic, yes, but in a strange way wise:
He made up words whose meanings were beneath
The words. Like "burden," which he told us meant
A mustache, or the door knob which he deemed
A fly knob (Closed you'll keep the flies all pent
Up outside), then muttered that he dreamed
Of being free himself. He went to court
Where novice lawyers asked the date, the place
(he knew) but Bill, where do you live?—a snort—
it threw him—You know, I own the inter-space!
We never spoke of what the lawyers did.
To no one Billy cried, "I'm a sad kid."

7.

Attendings varied in their patient skills.
When Billy S. once called a girl a "wiggle,"
A snort erupted, though his lips were still,
From Dr. King, and then became a giggle.
When Dr. Hunt, the psychiatric chief,
In front of twenty students smiled and talked
To Billy S., utter disbelief
Shone from our puzzled faces; we were shocked
That Dr. Hunt had not made Billy sound
As nutty as he was; did he not know?
The issue's not that Billy's mind confounds
His thoughts, like a fearful cricket in the snow;
He's well-related and coherent, too,
So why embarrass him in front of you?

8.

His slippered feet bounced lightly on the floor,
He smoothed his white and thinning hair again,
His voice was low. I tried gently to explore
The dejection that was his gloomy den.
That sounds so hard, you look so sad, I said,
And waited patiently for him to speak,
And waited, while his eyes stared, blank, ahead.
An hour passed; it felt more like a week.
Next time we met, I ditched the empathy:
What caused you to end up here, on this ward?
Was it sadness, or despair, or just ennui?
His hostility to me was my reward.
For to my resident he made it known
That he would not converse with me alone.

9.

He made a friend there, Mr. Grover Grant,
A large man, with a thick and slowed-down speech.
It sounded like the creepy kind of pant
He must have made when he made children screech.
The two of them spent all their time together:
Did they talk about their hopes and dreams and thoughts,
Or comment on the changes in the weather?
It warmed my heart to watch: no more distraught
Was he. He put on street clothes, wore a tie,
And painted, played the drums, and molded clay.
But he wouldn't look at me straight in the eye
Until I told him it was my last day.
He stared right at me, and was far from grieving.
I think he was quite pleased that I was leaving.

10.

The six-week session finished, I looked back
And asked myself if I had done some good
For these poor patients. Had it helped to talk
About their feelings? Had they understood
My empathy? I'd thought that was the key
For healing. But not with Grover's friend,
Whose cold demeanor, like a chilly sea,
Was an inaccessible beyond.
And Mr. Diaz, Billy S., were too
Far gone in worlds of sex, of made-up words.
That must be hard, would likely help undo
Not despair or stress, but things absurd.
For psychiatry I'd had high hopes;
I changed my focus now to stethoscopes.

Spirit of Mania

He chuckles in the corner at an empty table
Grinning wide,
From the voice inside his mind,
And laughs up a spirit from his belly,
To drift a foot above his head,
In vanilla-scented streams
With round, ruddy cheeks,
Eating ice cream and wearing silver rings,
Chuckling with sticky fingers,
'Til Laughing Buddha
Chuckled up, now hanging near the ceiling,
Sweeps its mists below my nose
Beneath my booted sole
To make me hop and tickle,
To find the pot of glee
Inside of me that bellows out
And joins the search for ice cream
And starched shirttails to untuck.

※ *Stephanie Snow*

Reflections on Spring Becoming

Today, on my first day on General Surgery Ward 9B,
I ventured down a hallway, scalpel in hand
to relieve a sweet old lady of a Jackson-Pratt drain.

She lay in the same bed you had a year before
when we saw the first snowfall—it was a Saturday evening—
through the windows of the Victoria General Hospital.

The evening the first snow fell you told me when you got out,
when you were well again, you would photograph me
sitting on the steps of the antique store across the street
wearing a green sweater amidst the snow. You kissed me
in front of Robert Pope's painted figures. You, me
and your IV an incongruent threesome, mirrored in art.

You never did take that picture of me,
And now the snow is gone.

Foley

As a kid you pissed
your name in the snow; at sixteen
you showed it to a girl
for the first time, face damp
and flushed. Now wires
thread your body.
I pull your old penis
from the fat seat of your thigh
and hold tight
as the catheter slides in to let
the blood and urine out,
tubing taped to your leg,
your glorious moment passed—
my first one.

※ *Sachin B. Patel*

Call Room

Seldom are there beautiful sunsets in call rooms,
only the quiet hum of a hospital heating system,
ambulance echoes bouncing between buildings,
the vibration of my fatigued pager.

I feel the passion I had for life's little things
slowly fading away. My love of Hitchcock films
and moonlit walks are squeezed out of me
leaving only brooding,
and my pedantic obsession
with getting the answer right and impressing
the attending with my five-minute presentation.

A ten-year-old boy who presents with a history of violent behavior
and a chief complaint of "My dad beats me."

How can I convey in my brief five minutes
the insanity of his father
who, after eight years of being violated in jail, can only show his
affection by grabbing a belt to beat the love into his child's flesh and
              blood?

Will five minutes be enough to tell my attending
that I haven't seen my mother for weeks
because I read articles on sepsis before pre-rounds.
And that I miss the sizzling samosas of home,
devouring, instead, soggy cafeteria french fries to stay awake.

Under the shadows of call-room bulb,
my heavy lids close. The hospital walls dissolve
and I float past abandoned factories
hearing holy songs from an old church,
songs that become hymns to my deceased patients

as I march alongside their coffins to a graveyard
where society's forgotten are buried.

A meth addict I once treated
weeps beside a tombstone.
She's lost a mother, a husband, a baby girl
to the illness of poverty.

Her story flashes past me like
the rush of bubbling crank racing
through her veins as she tries to erase the memory
of having to sell her body to buy a guitar
for her little boy's birthday, unable to erase
the shame she felt when that guitar
became currency for her next hit.
She didn't mean it, she swore to me,
her maternal love not enough
to stop the syringe from piercing her vein.
Her red eyes search the overcast sky for salvation.

My pager leaps to life with a piercing scream,
I am called to the nursery.
A seven-day-old infant shivers in the incubator.
His teenage parents have abandoned him,
and all I can do is stroke his apple-sized head and mumble a lullaby,
fighting my own tears of helplessness.

How is five minutes enough
to present these stories?
Each a pearl connected by a divine thread.

If through medicine I'm connected to humanity,
then why am I so disconnected from myself?
Why do I go home numb, unable to talk
to the ones I love about what I've seen?
All I feel is tired . . . I want to run away
from myself.

My peers feel it too.
We write orders for medications we don't fully understand.
We reassure patients that we will do our best to help them
when we know that tomorrow could be their last sunrise
when we should tell them to cast their eyes
toward the magnificent orb on the horizon,
because they may never see it again.
But instead I ask the patient if he has any pain
—I have to get my presentation ready.
Now tell me, how can I convey all that in five minutes?

Exhausted, I sit here with the humming vents
the morning sirens.

I survived the night.

There are no answers to human suffering.
Just my chance to help
create sunrises when there is only darkness,
and sing lullabies to life's forgotten children.

Gazing over the horizon
past the glimmering glass skyscrapers
deep into a glowing winter morning
I see a beautiful sunrise
countless others in this building may never see.

The Breast

The woman who spoke no English
found a big lump in her breast,
so off she went to the hospital
to have the issue addressed.
The doctors would cut out a piece of it,
so far as she could perceive.
They'd examine the lump for cancer
and say if she'd stay or leave.

When she awakened, to her great horror,
there was only a scar on her skin.
She waited for someone to tell her
what happened where once breast had been.

At six o'clock every morning,
a group of young doctors would come.
They would glance at her half-empty chest,
change the bandage and leave with a hum.
On the day that they gave her clothes back,
came her niece, away for a spell.
She was the only one in the family
who could understand English well.
The niece was angry and shaken
that nothing had been discussed;
they had handed her aunt a paper,
which she had signed with credulous trust.
I had helped at the operation,
watched the knives of the surgeons begin.
With scissors and sutures they snipped
and cut and tied up the bleeding skin.
I'd held the breast, tattered and heavy,
to keep it out of the field.
Its swirly reds and yellows
slowly began to yield.

A last slice and down dropped the breast
into a pan shaped like a square.
Save an ellipse of nippled skin
it resembled some Italian fare,
with tomato sauce and mozzarella,
about to be baked, just prepared.
Plopped uncooked onto the table,
nobody noticed or cared.
Like a group of chefs serving their guest
an impressive but unfinished platter,
the surgeons did all of the technical work,
but failed to say what was the matter.
No one told the aunt what had happened,
no one said what was wrong with her breast.
To remove it of course meant cancer—
they simply assumed she had guessed.

※ *Karen Wilson*

Signs

Hands—palm tree fronds fluttering in a windstorm
Assigning silent meaning I do not understand:
a ballet obscure, hands chalk-white, thin,
ragged nails and torn skin, workers; no pretense
of the manicured. I talk to her, watch her face,
as she looks past my shoulder. And from behind
I hear the ventriloquist parrot.

When I examine her hands she cannot speak.
As I come close, check her throat, a whisper
of wind trails my neck and I wonder
if she is talking behind my back.

First Suture

The mother shakes
but the child flails
with terror
a four inch gash
on her perfect brow
The father waits outside
pacing, raging
his answer to fear
Hold her
still please
My junior hand
trembles under taut rubber
to small choking sobs
My needle much too close
to that sea-blue eye
Her mother sings a lullaby
to calm us
It goes in and out until
I cut the last knot.

My Classic Psych Patient

The patient showed classic symptoms,
humming Beethoven's 5^{th,}
dressed in a ruffled shirt, a white wig,
brown coat with tails, tight white stockings
below short pants.
Been here longer than me.
We dress him from the shop on 4th
to stop him raving, Nurse Matty smiled,
in her own costume of cat-and-dog scrubs, cartooned,
comfortable clothing without the boat hat
my fiancée's grandmother would have demanded
instead of this disgrace.
I skip his three-tomed file of past treatments, failures,
disciplinary actions, side effects,
notes, long and monotonous,
poured over by predecessors.
He asked my name and
I answered Benjamin Springfield.
A good American name.
He asked where I was from and
I answered Central Jersey.
He asked what town and
I answered Piscataway.
I'm from Franklin, Mr. Benjamin
so I'll call you by the great inventor's name—
a man I know well fighting those Bastard Brits.
I asked why. Liberty, he replied,
and we talked tirelessly
through my noon lecture
over a cobblestone trail of conversation.

Mary Fletcher Hospital, 1958

Deep cold. Late at night
the ward is dim. Cousin, like kid sister,
in the starched gray dress of a student nurse,
you stand behind the low desk, phone in hand,
flushed, looking out
over the double row of beds. My white-buck
soles creak down the polished floor,
palpating the tile like a native
on the hunt. I breathe out through my
teeth. Me, night call doctor? No, just another
student, third-year medical, starched white,
and green.
              We were it, 2:00 A.M. Intern,
resident in bed, charge nurse down the other hall.

A woman, dusky as the ward, breathes deeply,
bubbles froth at her lips.
Let's turn up
the oxygen, I say, for want of something
more clever. You speak her blood pressure and pulse.
Her eyes seem to turn inward, searching
for breath. We tip up the head of her bed,
you suction her mouth. She turns her head
to you in gratitude and lowers her lids
over vacant eyes.
              The room becomes
silent but for a chorus
of hushed breathing. Wind
whines through cracks in the window frames. Snow
brushes the glass. One hand in mine,
one in yours she quiets
and goes to sleep.

Fishing

Water fills the mind at night in
slow minutes
                before dawn.

A wearied surgeon flaps his eyelids
gently closed, then opened wide
like the wings of butterflies.

Suture drawn from paper sleeves
sweeps in arcs like fishing line
cast to depths in split flesh
with curved hooks glinted.

Outside, leaves swim
to the ground, directed

by the breeze
                like a school of fish.

※ *Michael Doo*

Topsy-Turvy

Even such systematic distraction—Fun Centers,
polka-dotted curtains, clowns roaming the halls—
cannot disguise the fact that this
is a place very different than home.

In this place, open all night, lives are measured
in tempos of four, and eight, and twelve, and
a legion of healers, clad in cartoon creatures, toils
in a perpetually still undersea world.

It perplexes, Jerry Springer and Martha Stewart
preaching to a sleeping child,
while amidst a steady background of voices,
chirps, beeps, and clicks,
a cadence of cries beats on—

Welcome to Miller Children's,
where among the smallest are giants,
not a place for a child to be.

5 A.M. **poem**

i fall asleep on the floor
on the couch
against your chest
in bed
in class
in the car
on the plane
across two chairs
in your arms
i enjoy sleeping
though I may be maligned

for indulging in that simple pleasure, and
others

Patience, for M.S.

Mary has fired you, her physician, many times, once last week while I
      was away on vacation, but already she has hired you again.
Why don't you send her elsewhere? Who needs her show business
      histrionics, her bitterness and offhand complaining
about her cardiologist who has it out for her, and her
      otolaryngologist who is single-handedly responsible for the
      deterioration
of her once famous voice? You showed me the sepia-toned
      photographs from her radio days, in tribute to a faded star,
and it's shocking those eyes behind her boxy senior citizen shades
      were once vibrant and wild, but I see you smile when
she shows up in the office, even if it is three times a week without an
      appointment, saying this time she almost
fell over in the street and, incidentally, has had the best bowel
      movement she's had in two full years of frustration, firm and
      substantial.
She calls you in the middle of the day with problems about her
      laxatives and tranquilizers and you roll your eyes at me and
      swing your head
to the side in the same gesture I might have made as a teenager on
      the phone with a parent, indulgent and intolerant.
Next week, she's in the waiting area before you've gotten back from
      lunch, and I reintroduce myself. She tells me of her young
singing student, a single businessman of sixty who knew her name,
      who has no patience to sing songs that will train his voice,
      difficult songs,
but you've got to practice and use the nuance and passion of your
      voice to make plain songs pretty, and that, she says, is how to
      sing.

※   *Beth Seltzer*

A Day in the Life

I haven't seen the sun in days.
It's still dark, no problem finding a parking space.
I enter the building carrying clipboard and white coat
Blinking, as the fluorescents hit my face.

The surgery team stands in the ICU, 5:30 A.M.,
Halfway through a month of sixteen-hour days.
Later, winter light filters through unopenable windows
As we move from patient to OR to patient in the hospital maze.

Through the window in the visitors' lounge
The sun catches the team's eyes as we pass
At the end of the day five residents, one medical student
pressed to the glass.

※ *Neeta Jain*

When the Blood Fell Short of Her Toes

I would advise my mother the
same if the blood fell short of her
toes, the anesthesia doctor tells.

The useless leg, staining rouge, sits in
the crook of my arm. I brace it,
the knee's right angle corners my
elbow in my hip
                which bruises later.

She cannot endure intubation
from the weakness in her beat,
eyeliner straight-edged below
a cloudy clean cap. We search

at her ischium
with numbing sticks, rooting
to quiet the sharpness of nerves.

My gut crumples
                with her face.

I'll make you a nice wooden one,
her husband catches their tears
on his big thumb.

※ *Richard M. Berlin*

Inside Out

Still fresh
with the smell of aftershave,
he sprawls in bed,
seersucker johnny worn backwards,
wrapped in plastic.
He knows the date, the hospital,
can name Clinton, Bush, Reagan.
Ribbons lie on his nightstand
where a gift box holds a paisley
gown, sleeve pulled inside out.
He lifts the box,
eyes ricocheting
from mine to the robe
as he lunges an arm
at the turned-in sleeve.
Another lunge, another,
his arm sliding into air
as he shoves me away,
two men alone in a room,
helpless to reverse
a world pulled inside out.

※ *Richard M. Berlin*

Teamwork

I was just a student doing scut work
with my Senior Resident when the call came in—
an ER patient in shock and a Charge Nurse
who needed a diagnosis. He dropped
the phone and we both started running—
he smelled a ruptured triple A
and we knew that surgery, STAT,
was the only chance for a save.
We careened down fourteen flights
like two boulders in a bobsled chute,
the Senior barking our game plan,
and we arrived at a blue body gasping
through a face mask, a single IV
dripping like a bad faucet, the Charge Nurse
in the corner stroking her stethoscope
with an alcohol swab, relaxed as a woman
polishing a silver service for twelve.
I called the OR as the Senior strapped
the patient down and ordered the nurse
to pull the lines. But she just glared,
lifted the phone, and called her supervisor,
the Senior whirling like a kung fu fighter,
grabbing the IV bag, ripping down x-rays,
releasing the brakes, and smashing
the cart through the swinging doors,
the treatment room behind us littered
with severed lines and plastic tubes,
the nurse's scream chasing us down the hall:
Fucking assholes! You fucking assholes!

✳ *Richard M. Berlin*

Surgery Rotation

The last weak rays of sun
shine on the drab-green chart room walls.
The evening staff has finished report,
and the wing quiets as night comes on,
our team reviewing the final tasks
on our thirty-six-hour shift—
a dressing for a gangrenous toe,
x-rays to read, IVs to start.
The surgeon opens an aluminum chart
with two hundred colored pages
clipped by a spring, pink for progress
notes, blue for vital signs, lab values
stapled in like tattered rags
on a scarecrow. He points the cold
metal at me like an accusation,
and lets it fall just before I get my grip.
I can still see it tumble
like a cannon ball Galileo dropped
from the Leaning Tower,
and I can still hear it explode
on the linoleum floor,
pages scattered like straw in a thunderstorm.
But what I remember best is how hard
the floor felt against my knees,
the dust balls in the corner,
the way no one moved
to help me pick up the pages,
the shined black toes of the surgeon's shoes.

Frank Edwards

Heal Me, Doctor

Six A.M. teaching rounds with Dr. Morgan,
we semicircle the bed.

Here we are, my dear.
The roosters, again.
How'd you sleep?
Any pain?
Breathing well?
Like goslings in short white coats
we imprint the mood.

It's Alan's turn.
He clears his throat,
introduces himself.
Aware of Morgan and his
knowledge of the spleen,
he palpates first her sunken abdomen,
gestures grandly,
then helps her sit.

His stethoscope skips from side to side
down her Quasimodo back. Vertebrae
jut like spires. Laying her down, he directs
his auscultation to the front.

Five feet away
we hear her failing heart
balloon the skin between her ribs
where the breast is missing.
Something else draws our eyes
chestward to Alan.
The earpieces of his shiny Littmann
ring his neck, disengaged,
a shaman's amulet.

Morgan's face stays priestly.
Halfway across the heart,
Alan stops and straightens.
His forehead moist,
he clears his throat again.

Mrs. Smith, would you mind if I listened to you
a different way now?
I don't mind, she says.
Yes indeed, says Morgan.
Splendid idea.

The dying woman does not see
Alan slip the prongs
into his ears,
but she smiles along
with our laughter,
floats in it,
eyes closed.

※ *Sarah Jane Cook*

NG Tube

Eyes watery and small.
A mouth full
of chalky growths and white ulcers,
mucus-pooled.

We slip the greased tube into her right nostril,
blood begins to ooze.
I hear the first real words gurgle from
that mouth—
Oh my god.

We can't get in.
We pull it out.
Tears drip down her
thin, drooping skin.

We try the other side.
Cough, gag,
it curls in the white pasty mouth.
Gag again, pull back.
Push,
it goes down.

She looks me in the eyes.

Meghann Kaiser

Catching Comprehension

I am referring to her in the masculine.
Too late to catch myself,
I can't remember the words to apologize.
I hope she understands.

Legs slouch spread-eagle, feet propped up.
Knees bend awkward at eye level with me
with the drape strung out between them
fluttering in time with the air conditioner
like the makeshift blanket stage of a second-grade puppet show.
I cower in the corner opposite,
beneath a burden of unrelenting English.
I know the words for head and back, but
Pap Smear?
¿Como se dice la cosa de que viene los bebes?

As she cranes her head forward,
her face wobbles into view.
She is reenacting her youngest son's birth.
I can't tell what happened when, or why, but
her face squints and pooches in the pains of communication.
My interpretation insufficient for medical advice,
my hand comes to rest on her right ankle.
The sticky residue of fractured phrases,
and sweat, invests my palm.
No se, Señora.
I hope she understands.

Unnameable Galaxies

He grabs a model airplane kit
from the O.T.
inhaling its glue
then runs screaming
half-naked down the street,
two orderlies in pursuit.
They wrestle him down,
apply the straitjacket,
then pump a syringe full
of inertia into his thigh.
We are light-years away, watching

his centrifuge of human mind
slowly spin down
into the reality of its DNA
at the bottom of some test tube.
When the sine wave of reason
reaches its nadir, he crawls
into his black hole
and remains there.

Father once tried to beat,
then shame it out of him
as a watch ticked
next to his ear on the bedside table.
He turned to face the wall.
We were light-years away.

The Doghouse

I'll tell you what having a relationship in med school is like.

It's like having a dog and thinking to yourself,
He needs a doghouse but
Somehow there are always about a million other things to do,
Papers, tests, rounds, residency applications . . .

Until one day you get to feeling so guilty
You decide you're going build that doghouse
Come hell or high water, out of anything you can find,
Rulers, masking tape, newspapers, toilet paper tubes . . .

And then you have a doghouse.

Only every time your dog actually goes inside that house,
Or it rains, or the wind blows just a little too hard,
Or a possum breathes on it wrong, your little doghouse has to be
Propped up, picked up, retaped, repaired . . .

So that in time you start to wonder, why you have one at all.
It's not like any other doghouse. It does
Hardly any of the things you hoped it would. All your neighbors
Point, laugh, roll their eyes, shake their heads . . .

But every now and then

I get home at 7 o'clock in the morning after a night on call
Lie down in the dew grass on the lawn beside my dog,
In the shade of a makeshift doghouse.

Noah Raizman

Tumor, for R.R.

Great uncle Walt once spoke to me
through the mouthpiece of my father,

about the uncut hair of graves and now,
cornered by the dying, I pray to him,

Whitman, patron saint of exuberance
in the face of despair,

did he turn his back on us, just
long enough to sing a song of himself?

My family is dying, every day another one disappears.
My patient does not notice anymore when I am in the room.

He still stares at me, plangent,
the sad face of a dog,

and his family, like mine, will engage
a roundtable discussion of dignity,

grace, and resuscitation, which I have only
recently learned, and fear to practice.

Not there for burial, I visit, weeks later,
sun fresh on the first sprouts of grass,

delicate, pale tendrils poking up, and I pray
to Whitman, his tousled hair, his great

Dionysian beard, his golden chariot, to bring
new life from this ground, new sons from fathers,

and fathers from sons.

Stephanie Snow

Still Life

A game we played during our Bachelor of Arts:
Juxtaposing personal objects into a still life
Art catches a snapshot of becoming

I was pleased this evening to realize
that my latest portrait of self
contains a pair of red Birkenstock surgery shoes
well worn, well loved

Intern

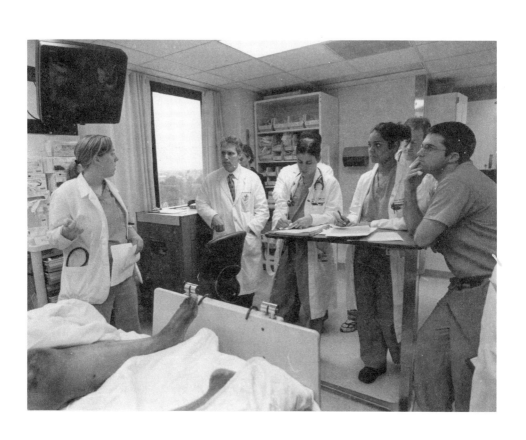

Emily R. Transue

Internship in Seattle

I moved to a city that is famous for its rain.
Mostly it drizzles,
sometimes it pours.

The people here don't use umbrellas:
it's considered gauche
to acknowledge the weather;
besides, in large numbers
they'd block out the sun
and create a public nuisance.

When I first came here I got wet a lot.

Then just recently
I got myself a raincoat;
It's made of shiny clear plastic.
It's invisible
against my skin;
and now I'm
always dry.

Nothing can get through.

Q4: The Call Cycle

1. On Call

Sometimes the busy moments
Are the easy ones.
Not the crazy times
When your pager keeps exploding
And the admits pour in
And the chaos unconcentrates
And you hope to hell you won't kill somebody
By mistake, distraction, oversight—
But the quiet moments are bad, too;
Too much time to think
To wonder when the next one's coming in
Whether you'll sleep the night through
Or get three hits at three A.M.
Time to be afraid of what you should've done and didn't
What you did do and should not have
In the wakeful silence, head on pillow.
The best times are
Just working, steadily,
Doing what is needed but not
More than can be done;
Riding the momentum of necessity,
Busy, numb.

2. Morning After

Green moss
Pebbles
A bit of broken glass;
Further off, a patch of yellow lichen.

It is so wet
And so clear
I'd swear that I can smell it through the glass,
That other world
Outside this window
Where I linger as the elevator dawdles.

After all these hours here
The smell of hospital is in my pores.
I wish the window opened.
I'd like to breathe the air.

3. Afternoon After

Have you ever been so tired
You could cry, just from fatigue?
So tired that voices hurt your ears
And you'd like to curl up in a little ball
Under a table or a rock
And die
If dying means to sleep forever.

4. The Day Between

My family thinks
If you're not "on," you're "off."

It's hard to argue
Harder to explain
That a day of work
With sleep before and after
Is luxury enough.

5. Pre

This morning I rounded on
Two patients in my care a month each
On ventilators,
Patients who have never spoken to me.
A woman whose abdominal pathology
All of modern medicine has failed to diagnose,
Another whose lymphoma all of modern medicine has failed to cure,
A third who will recover from her cellulitis,
Go home, shoot up again, come in again.

I was screamed at by the brother of a man
Who's dying of hepatic carcinoma at 41;
He yelled at me because he couldn't yell at God

Then I went to clinic, to see
A woman with diabetes without a home
Who's struggling against despair
And a man who wanted prescriptions
And someone to laugh at his jokes
And an alcoholic who needs a detox bed
But won't get one
Because the city has none empty.

I leave the radio off, driving home,
Because I cannot stand to hear another voice, another noise.
I sit on my sofa, still,
My mind a blank;
I am
An eggshell
Or a melon rind:
Scooped out,
Round and empty.
I've given all I have; there's nothing left.

I soak in a hot bath and go to sleep.

❋ *Mindy Shah*

Intensive Care

A get-well-soon balloon
hovers above the hiss
of the vent, calculated volumes
of gas to feed both
the balloon, your body.

Granddaughter's gift,
photos of the family
frame the rack
where the chart expands
with the epic of your death.

Pages dangle
where the holes
ripped through,
nobody bothers
to bind anything anymore.

Richard M. Berlin

First Night On Call, Coronary Care Unit

I'm driving a knife-edge
mountain ridge at midnight,
no lines, no guard rails,

a semi screaming down my lane
ready to crush me with its cargo
of science I still need to learn.

A rusted-out Chevy on my tail
scrapes an exhaust pipe and sends
sparks into darkness, their brief light

fading fast as facts I've memorized.
I don't know who will die tonight,
me or them, but I grip the wheel tight,

knuckles lit white by high beams,
my own heart pounding, heading up hill,
engine moaning, pedal to the metal.

Richard M. Berlin

The Hotseat

> *I swear by Apollo the physician, and Aesculapius,*
> *and Hygeia and Panacea, and all the gods and*
> *goddesses . . . to reckon him who taught me this Art*
> *equally dear to me as my parents . . .*
> —from the Hippocratic Oath

O700 and thirty housestaff collapse
like shipwreck survivors.
After 24 sleepless hours
of children renounced by Hygeia,
our eyes are drowned in shadow.
A few nod before he enters
ruddy-faced and rested,
white coat starched and spotless:
Dr. Harry, Chief of the Mecca,
diagnostic wizard, the power
who can crush careers with a word.
He slaps a chest film on the light box
and hooks a bleary intern:
Tell me, doctor,
what is the shape of this child's ears?
Fifteen seconds, thirty, a minute of silence,
sweat weeps from the intern's forehead.
Harry scorches him with questions
and solves the riddle like Aesculapius,
even kneads the intern's shoulders
as if soothing a bruise.
We curse him all day, stay awake
all night to earn his love,
and when we descend to Radiology
with our own tame students, we slap
a film on the light box and raise
their first beads of sweat.

※ *Kelley Jean White*

Deathbeds

An old man, frail, alone, emaciated; he fought in
World War I; he once shook the hand of the Prince of
      Wales

An anencephalic baby; her Cambodian mother speaks no
      English

A high school football player with viral myocarditis
and failure; he played in a game
      three days ago

A five-year-old Hispanic girl with long black curls
and a red velvet dress; a drug dealer
      swerved onto the sidewalk and crushed her against a
wall on Christmas Eve

A business man admitted for "elective" heart surgery;
I see his eyes change as the EKG deteriorates under
my hands

A fetus born at twenty-two weeks; its eyes are still
      fused

A pudgy blond baby carried, pulse-less, into the ER in
a fireman's arms; his drunk uncle passed out on top
      of him

A red-headed thirty-five-year-old mother of three,
vomiting blood;
      her family never knew she drank

A preschooler with leukemia late on Christmas day;

the priest has given last rights;
        the parents offer him the presents the child opened
that morning

A mildly retarded Mennonite girl with maple sugar
urine disease; her family is pleased
        to donate her organs—they know many people with genetic
        disease
They ask that we call their community now, at four A.M.:
They're farmers, they'll be awake, they'll want to

Toxic Environment

A six-inch laceration:
in the history (translated
by a guy from maintenance),
the mother blames the stepfather,
says she will try to get together
bus fare to Chicago,
get the hell out.
He is a big child for three;
twenty-seven stitches;
as I am finishing
there is a skirmish at
the double doors.
The stepfather is there,
a long blade glinting
in this right hand.
The security guards secure
his arms and I,
so brave, so righteous,
walk forward.
He drops to his knees
and embraces my legs:
Arrest me, punish me,
I did it. . . . The weapon is
a paint scraper.
He speaks good English:
The kid has lead poisoning.
I was scraping the wall
to repaint and he walked in
and started eating from
the pile of scrapings
on the floor. I lost control.
I flung it at him. I did it.
I did, but I love him,
I love the boy, I love

his mother, I was trying
to help. He crosses
himself. Lies face down
to await the police.

Lady Morphine

Through the moans and wheezing cries,
the sudden bursts of laughter near the coffee pot
at the end of the darkened hall,
the nurses call and Lady Morphine comes
or maybe me in my new white coat
learning the flickered rhythms of 3 A.M.
on the cancer ward, stumbling
and stunned from the idea of sleep,
the exquisite torture of pager beeps
killing charity and thought.

Primum non nocere; do no harm
and who's to say the harm of one less breath
against the crush of pain that breaks a man
who lived through Iwo Jima like Mr. C—
fifty-two and riddled, we both knew
the chemo wasn't helping, and still
I feel his rusted whisper up my neck.
Please, Doc, kill me. Please.
There's no one left to care.

Was it cowardice that answered? Or Moses—
the thought of his ragged breath as he was left
behind on the wrong bank of the Jordan
while a box of broken stone was rowed across?
So I gave Mr. C a few extra, careful drops
to hide him deep for hours. Enough or not
he thanked me later and who's to say . . .

※ *Richard M. Berlin*

On Call, 3 A.M.

After she pages me to pronounce him,
we pull the white sheet to his chin
in one quick movement, our eyes
on his, then locked on each other's.
We know what we want.
In the deserted call room
with its fresh linen and barren walls,
we smell each other in the darkness,
the sweat on our scrubs, antiseptic soap
on our fingers. We lick each other's salt
like deer ready to run the instant we are called.
We know how to strip a body fast,
our uniforms falling to the linoleum floor,
our pleasure like worn stones tumbling in the tide.
We know what pours from the sea
of our bodies will not be tested in the lab,
and what we say will not be recorded in a chart,
though our movements are as efficient
as any surgical procedure. And afterwards,
when we kiss and wash our hands again,
we smooth the sheets and pull them tight.
We even make hospital corners.

76

After years of riding a motorcycle
I have fallen in love with certain roads, even small segments.
For just a few seconds, near the 30th Street Train Station,
My helmet fills with the scent of baking donuts.
The air is warmer here, fighting off the morning chill.

The trial by hours of medical education, the five-to-nine grind,
Places me on this road during the predawn and evening batches.
I savor these moments,
A respite to the olfactory onslaught that lies ahead.
The bouquet of urine greeting me in the emergency department,
Breakfast trays with sickly sweet hospital pancake syrup
Melena of the ICU.
In the hospital, I try to forget how smell works—
Molecules of whatever dissolving in the moist linings of my nose,
Destined to be absorbed.

How nice it would be to convince the city's homeless to sleep by this
            road,
To soak up the perfume of chocolate sprinkles and glaze,
Then float off the street to the interns
Waiting to dunk something in coffee.

Resident

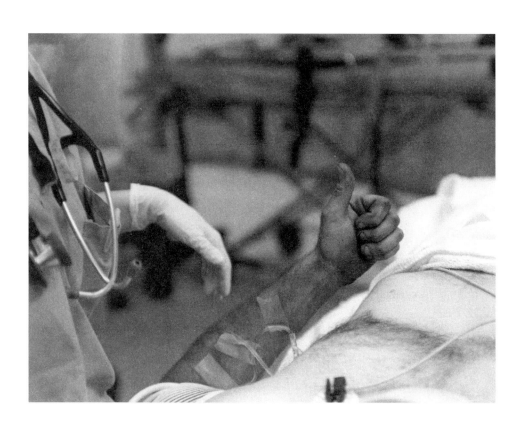

Richard M. Berlin

January Thaw

It is the winter of chest pain and snow,
all the drunks smashed
through the ER doors.

The Senior Resident in his new blue coat
can coax a silent heart,
but only curses the jaundiced men,

exiles them to frozen doorways,
shivered Thunderbird,
the lukewarm comfort of bitter coffee.

And he hates Drunken Johnny most of all,
loathes him and saves him,
Johnny rising immortal in disregard

for the slum of his body.
One night, he stumbles in, explosive,
ice loaded on his beard,

snow like soot falling from his flak jacket.
He shuffles to the gurney,
the Senior's rage like an ice storm.

Johnny's hands shake
to untie a glazed lace,
and when he grunts a drunken heave

on his boot, his foot breaks off
silent as torn moldy bread.
Johnny collapses, an intern vomits,

but the Senior stands hard
until tears kick across his face
and he wails like spring rain for a surgeon.

※ *Emily R. Transue*

Haiku of Residency

1. Please

Please do not code now;
I have just found a warm spot
in this cold hard bed.

2. Identity

Who am I to you?
White-coated figure folds cold hands,
calls in scripts by phone.

3. Hematemesis

We each have five pints
of blood. I counted your five
in the red basin.

4. Eight A.M.

You say good morning
but does it count as morning
if I did not sleep?

5. Alarm

My pager goes off
Searing explosion of noise
—No, that's a fire drill.

6. Code

Seven flights of stairs
Run breathless in double steps
My heart fast; yours, still.

Sick

A thirty-two-year-old with
alcoholic cirrhosis and
variceal bleeding.
TIPS last night
but couldn't get it in.
Needled through her liver for a
couple hours then called it
quits. Sedated. She's
still on the vent, probably
a surgical shunt.

As we turn to walk away I ask,
Where did she get the black eye?
Ran into a door, the intern says.

The next day he's gone,
I get called to see her boyfriend
who wants to talk to a doctor.
Will she be okay? he asks,
brown eyes dark, unreadable.
I say, I don't know.
I found her in a pool of blood,
he says. I know her liver's bad,
she knows it too, but she keeps
drinking. He looks at me,
but I don't answer. She's pretty sick,
he says uncertainly, and I say, Yes.
Will she be okay? he asks
and I say, I don't know.

MAO

It's what we call
a "soft" admit,
which means
your illness does not
impress us.
Here is your room,
the toilet, your bag
of personal belongings.
The toothbrush is
on us.
We'll round at seven,
but I can tell
by the smell of your breath
you're going to live.

Gratitude

Mr. H, taciturn and a little odd,
Whose wife preferred another man,
And who would come faithfully
Late by fifteen regular minutes
Each Friday. Mrs. V and her loyal
Veterinarian daughter, the other
An Internet mogul in Hawaii,
Who wanted only for us to spare
The eyebrows, though she'd lost
All sense of self and hair. These images
Are the ones I remember, when the
Clock runs two hours early,
And the waiting room shrinks to
Maximum capacity. The chocolate and the cards
Are nothing compared to this—a touching—
My hands weaving their way through a life,
Splayed out like tendons, tense and playable,
The sweetest and most bitter of chords.

October 1st

You ask about my day—
I should have taken a Polaroid:
lime curtains, black sheets,
yellow man, your age,
rusted nails on restless fingers,
pregnant belly with twisted purple veins,
afraid to ask for directions.

Said he drank to escape the loneliness.
That down escalator, no basement floor.

I hold his hand, breathe through my mouth,
discuss the facts from yesterday's spill;
a new liver, perhaps.

You ask about my day—
I tell you it was fine;
my side of the bed grows farther.

Catharine Clark-Sayles

Red Hill Is Dissolving

We awaken each morning to monstrous slides gone.
At work in the ICU gray rain drizzles windows,
and the creek runs sullen with mud. Even the white
heron draggles dirt stains, and I minutely adjust
each IV—Mr. C. slides further each day
though teams of consultants make plans.

In the break room we form in committees, sign
petitions to save Red Hill, but not everything
wants to be saved, and salvation may come rattling
a can for loose change as we say we have given
enough, never knowing how high the tab runs.

We forget the weird beauty in red rivulets
coursing gouged clay, their convergence in streams
below—a pink froth of mud and white oleander
blossoms spinning toward the sea.

Doing Time

For four months I swabbed number five mirrors,
looked in the back of their throats, breathing
what they exhaled, all of them one collective breath,
the lifers, rapists, innocents, petty thieves.
Bright orange splashed across the yards,
basketballs stopped thumping midway to stare,
endless lapping of the track ceased.

Past the holding cages, the smell of coffee and sweat,
the cackling, the "hey baby"s, all the time,
my eyes like those of the southernmost seals,
no visible pupil, just black glass, reflecting,
a shield where nothing could penetrate,
weak enough only to see them as one
vilified, teeming mass, cockroaches in my mulch pile,
something the soul turns over with a pitchfork to see.

Two guards flanked him, but no file.
They told me anyway he cut a woman, a nurse,
into pieces, and threw her in the Olentangy
after he'd taken his fill of her, and now,
just as precisely, he's written me a letter
on how "egregiously" I've treated him
looking at his "orifices," probing, not explaining.
When I leave, a nurse is raped,
a pointed bedspring held against her throat. For years
I can only hear him laughing,
uncaged, free to breathe, fomenting.

County Trauma

Squirt her
my chief resident orders

18 years old, chest smashed into the steering wheel
a crescent-shaped bruise between her breasts

Squirt her

push dye into her veins
outline her aorta arching off the heart
see if she's got a tear

flat on the gurney
wild-eyed, No, no, she repeats
I don't want it

he forces the gurney out of the trauma unit
into the hallway, down to X-Ray
I pull at the front, an accomplice,
the get-away driver

If your aorta's ripped your chance of surviving
is a goose-egg, he says, then
bends his thumb and index finger to form
a perfect circle, a zero

No, no, she repeats
I don't want it

we push faster

Attending

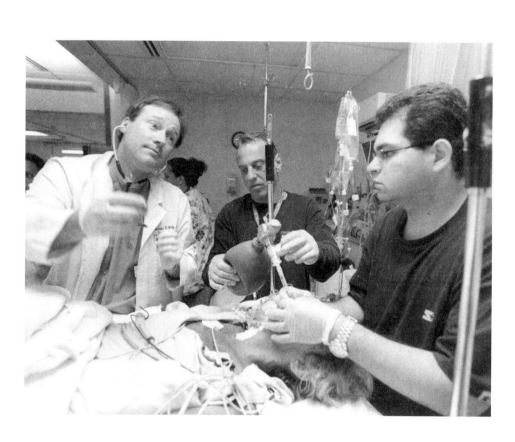

Cases

Man in his late seventies comes in with his wife,
weak, lost twenty-five pounds, can't eat, hard to talk,
seeing double off and on past eighteen months,
been to a family doctor and two specialists.

They don't know, I've got some ideas. It's
beyond my scope, here in the rural north country.
I get him tucked away in the medical center
by the following morning. He's out in five days

with a diagnosis, I was right for once. He's
eighty percent better on treatment, says
he's two hundred percent. Gives me the credit
for once. The gray hair helps. Man comes in

to emergency with loss of vision in one eye.
works full-time, in his sixties. It goes away
and he wants to go home. Internist and eye doctor
find nothing. I find something and say, No.

Family says I'm overreacting but they all agree,
reluctantly. Urgent angiogram—surgery on the
neck arteries is booked for the following morning.
That night his opposite side becomes paralyzed.

Emergency surgery cleans out a nearly
blocked vessel. They don't appreciate the
postoperative pain. They don't appreciate my
style or anything about me. He walks out

saved from an almost certain permanent
disability. Woman comes in with a headache,
high blood pressure, in her fifties. I do a spinal,
few red cells, radiologist gets me on the phone.

He says the CAT scan's negative, I'm not
so sure and send her down country for an
angiogram. Radiologist was right and I was
wrong—no aneurysm in her brain. Young

mother of two comes in with seizures hard to
control all her life, and paralyzed on the right side
from birth. I consider a CAT scan a waste of money:
the gray hair stands for experience, remember?

She gets slowly worse over the years. Her family
doctor does a CAT scan, finds a malformation
of the brain. We just ain't so smart, my old
teacher used to say when I was an intern. A man

comes in, in his sixties, can't work, losing weight,
muscles are twitching, hard to swallow, hard
to talk. Do some tests, tell his wife and him
he's got Lou Gehrig's Disease, it will affect

his breathing, he's going to die, it will be
tough, we'll try some things. We do, he gets
worse, can't walk, can't feed himself.
I visit the house: a small cape with a screened

porch behind a variety store in a small town in
New Hampshire. He gets worse, I
visit some more, talk some to him,
to his wife and son, the man dies.

※ *Emilie Osborn*

Stolen Kisses

The fresh-laundered smell
of a boy's shirt
startles me
leaning closer
with my stethoscope
I pretend to hear a murmur
soak in the odor
of a kiss
at sixteen.

※ *Emilie Osborn*

Breast Exams

As we paddle across the bay, moonlight reflects
white floating plates, small as coins,
moon jellies. My patients' breasts
lie flat as I feel for seeds grown amuck,
malignancies in microcalcifications.
I press the soft convexities
between my fingers in a circular massage.
We talk of children, mothers, menopause,
cancer risks calculate in my head,
moon jellies floating on the bay.

※ *David Watts*

How Will They Take Me

she says, after they
see me. She
has a point, thin
as a diagnosis,
no admission
committee I know
would be pleased, if,
as she says, she
even got
the interview. How

does she do it, sitting
in my chair like a young
girl talking
about chemistry and medical
school and in the
same breath the time
her mother threw her
down the stairs.

Which mind am I
talking to? I say. She smiles
and turns the mind
inside out to the one
which resists logic
which was the country
I was coming from.

Of course.

It wasn't in her chart, the part
about the two minds
and how they know each other
but do not speak. Make

yourself listen, I say. And she
just smiles.

We argue about her weight
but the argument slimes
over us like mucus
over the unfed grumble
of her stomach. Both of us
were nauseous from that.
She brings in her mother
who corrects everything
she says, the same
mother who thought her daughter
made her boyfriend
disappear. And she smiles
for her mother as she keeps on
losing weight. Don't you

see the anger, I say,
the punishment?
It was the other mind
which said no, but it wanted
my help, would I
fix her constipation, fix
her pain, would I
make an appointment for
colonoscopy? She

never came for that. She showed up
less and less. And I
wondered if I had done enough
which is, I suppose, what one
always wonders
when someone dies
still wanting something from you.

Skin

I entered your home
shed my white coat
removed my shoes.

Soft broadloom met bare summer feet.

I sat on your carpet
a diabetic foot in my hand
on a summer's day

I thought your wound would heal.

Writing the note I realized I didn't feel
for a pulse, or test for sensation.

I blame the broadloom
your foot in my hand
its warmth.

Loving, Meticulously

He's swallowed bedsprings and screws,
batteries and coins, and most of a band radio.
All but his brains have been extracted.
The warden puts him in a cell with a blanket,
four walls and a light bulb swinging from a wire.
The light hypnotizes him into breaking it.
With the precision of a schoolboy arranging marbles,
he coats the jagged shards with bits of gum.

He feasts on Wrigley-coated glass, his ruse d'être,
followed by a bumpy, windowless ride to the ER,
hands and ankles cuffed.
The gowning and bloodletting and probing
make him feel alive again.
Counting backwards by sevens, he skips eighty-six
sinking under an ether halo.
I am laughing derisively

at us fools in white coats labeled with degrees,
cloaked in our own pomposity,
thinking we can save what he cares least about.
I am surrogate mother surgeon
plucking glass from his insides.
Peering down a long tube into his very darkness,
I am touched, loving him meticulously
in his acts of desperation.

Holding

for Pat

I ask you, Is there anything you want?
When you say, I want to live, I skip a breath
as if I'd fallen hard. You say, I'm sorry.

I'm not good at this, as if death is a skill anyone learns.
I want to say you should shout, rage, sow salt
across your pillow top, but I take your hand

watch the slow meander of morphine-soaked
thought slip away from the one, enormous thing
to distraction: wills, insurance, who will take the cats.

Hiss of oxygen, click of IV, all the useless trappings
I've hung around your bed, being human and unable
yet to find acceptance in the sway of trees

outside the window and the patch of sun
that tracks the minutes across your floor.
For a fierce and timeless moment I pray:

for miracles, for gentleness, for folding in.
We sit in silence and when you shake with tears
there is nothing but to hold you until the end.

The Recovery Room Veteran

darts furtive glares
as if the enemy skulks just beyond my shoulder

emergence delirium is too polysyllabic, too refined
for thrusts of fear
anger
flail

Mr. Pullman, you're in the recovery room now!
Lie back, you're okay!
Everything's all done!
(what's his first name?) David? Dave, lie back!

Are you hurting?

a spit of the eyes, face to face
     his search is futile
     we're unearthly, untrustworthy

I was a doctor once, Mr. Pullman says suddenly
surprising us with coherence or confabulation

we roll back on our heels; release our grips
the nurse comments, sotto, Aren't doctors always doctors?

I shrug, but know she's right
like a mother's always a mother, even after time
     crusts the raw-lipped nightmare of a child's death

the anesthesia resident begins report:
Fifty-eight-year-old man with a history of multiple suicide attempts . . .

recovery doesn't mean scarless

at discharge, his feet are crossed
his hands doze on the hospital linens;
as I sign the chart: *awake, alert, breathing well*
I casually ask Mr. Pullman his line of work—

Repairs, he says, and smiles as if beckoning a friend.

❋ *Jerald Winakur*

He Still Whistles

They come every four months
he smiles, drools, sits quietly
always says yes, only says yes

she bitches and sighs, bemoans
and cries, He's getting worse
he's only getting worse . . .

She can't take it anymore
and neither can I.
Have you considered a Home? I ask

prying into her blubbery folds
trying to discern what's inside
looking into her ruined

mascara-caked eyes
red and wrinkled now beyond relief
When she shyly says, Doctor,

I've gotten so fat . . . but do you know
he still whistles when
I take off my clothes . . .

and he sits there smiling, smiling
grinning, nodding
Yes, he says. Yes.

✳ *Renee Rossi*

Today's List of Denials

The sparrows that nest in the laundry exhaust spit out their rejected young onto the cement below, filmy eyes bulging like flies, little beaks open with silent cries, as mother passes them over again and again to bring food to her healthy young.

The chief cardiac surgeon walks by our operating room several times each day during bypass to smoke while the fellows build new coronaries for the two-pack-a-day smoker lying on the table.

And you and I—we eat Chinese take-out with our bare hands as we talk about ruptured aortas and units of blood while the Bosnian ex-mine sweeper with three bullet holes in his belly fastens down our granite slab countertops, shiny verde maughs, to hide our imperfections.

The Anatomy of the Hand

A long time ago when I was married
my husband, the plastic surgeon, came home
from the hospital late one night with a human
hand wrapped in newspaper like a fish.
There had been an urgent amputation,
a tumor of the forearm that did not affect
the hand. The patient wished to contribute
to the advancement of science. It was thought
that perhaps my husband could use the hand
in study. At first he placed it in the freezer
but being concerned that the babysitter
might inadvertently unwrap it he moved it
to a pickle jar filled with preserving fluid. It sat
downstairs on his workbench among paint
cans and assorted screws, another project
not finished or truly quite begun.
Even I would be taken in occasional surprise
turning with a basket of clean laundry, headed
for the steps. It must have been quite
difficult on the sitter. It waited.
Like an extreme merit badge project:
woodworking, fire craft, skeletal finger lore.
At first it was fat, swollen, but month by month
it aged, skin bleached, nails yellowed, bits of
skin frayed. I wondered at the status
of tendons and tendon sheaths, at the
(I hoped) preservation of the majestic,
magnificent, miraculous, angelic mechanism
by which the fingers tap. It was the left
hand. Tonight I wonder: Did it
hold a child? Did it wear a wedding
band? Did it touch a man? What work did it do?
Knitting? Typing? Filing? Weeding? Did it play
the piano? Did it bake bread? I do not want

to think of the woman, alive; I see her
body unwieldy like mine, the thin
cotton print dress, the empty sleeve. Or worse
I see her dead of the tumor and buried, bereft, while
the jar's top is thick with dust and cobwebs.
It became a mummy's hand, curling, reaching for the door,
the children brought their friends, switched
off all but a flashlight, ran screaming away,
delighted.
It is a long time since I lived there. I do not know
where the hand is now. He may have thrown it away. Alone
I wish it the dignity its service should command.

Solstice

The last time I can remember that my husband showed
love for me it was like this:
he was kept late at the hospital; when he came home
I was walking the dog at midnight on the November
street; he hurried to take the leash from me, pushed an arm
around my shoulder—
There's a madman loose in the city preying on women
alone.

His case was this: two women had been killed and a
third damaged, quite probably beyond hope.
The assailant's modus was to approach
a woman working alone in a small shop,
smash her head with a brick, and empty the cash register.
The first was at a dry cleaners, the second
a mom & pop store, the third was a young woman
working in her family's flower shop.
The florist was alive. They had her in surgery for
hours, picking skull fragments
from her brain. My husband, as plastic surgeon on
call, was asked to tuck what remained of her left ear
beneath a flap of skin:

later, it could be reconstructed,
later, if she survived. It felt trivial, while the
neurosurgeons labored and orthopedics
pinned bone and general surgeons stabilized bowel and
spleen, but he did as asked.
He followed her case closely though her management
was not in his hands.
Remarkably, she showed small signs of improvement,
a hint of recognition for her husband, her small son. Quite

uncharacteristically, he went with me to Quaker meeting.
He sat stirring beside me. I could see the tremble,
the push that they say comes
from God to lead one to speak. He struggled.
I thought he would stand. I watched his face, heard his
breath quicken. He wanted to speak of miracles and
hope. Of the small things we do, seemingly empty,
that may mean more than we can dream. The leading
never cleared. The hour closed. They asked for those
new to meeting to stand.

And a young woman rose in the front row, thin, knit
cap pulled over shaven head and hidden ear, that
woman rose and spoke her name.

Catching Up

we're gulping wine and
breathing garlic
underneath an awning
at an outdoor table on
a corner at the café in
the village
where my daughter
wraps spaghetti strands
around a fork and sprinkles
little questions
like the cool
prism drops
that end a scorching drought.
her brother's
suicide a ripple
in some distant galaxy
had choked her
into years of silent rage
but almost out of college now
she looks at me and knows
we need to talk.
once more I am
an intern
waiting for a chance
to cure somebody when
through swinging double doors
a fat man wheels into the ER
bawling as he clutches at his chest
and then gets quiet
and then gets very dark and blue.
as if my first dead patient
wasn't bad enough
I have to tell his wife and
all I do is put his glasses in her hand

without a word.
in the glow of laughter
from the tables all around us
as Chianti surges through me
I surprise myself
and suddenly begin to cry.

Any Calcification

A bone-white glow
the quality of clinical antiseptic
lights her face.

She is peering through a huge
magnifying glass
at the little white clumped
and clustered spots, gathered
like moon craters
after a meteor storm.

Any calcification is new calcification
until proven otherwise,
she said.

      And I thought
of the little breast cells—
after the slug
of hormones we used to try
and get pregnant—IVF,
clomaphen, egg donation,
pregnancy and nursing—
dying and getting calcified.

There are rules,
the radiologist said.
It can't be called *probably benign*
because that's less than two percent. This
is less than ten percent. She paused
then answered the unasked question: It needs
Mag Spots and a Core biopsy.

Lucille, Lucinda . . . I was thinking
of the time I gave them names, amazed

how they floated
there, suspended
in their own softness, a beauty
that defied the laws
of physics. It isn't a question
you said, of will we make
love, it's when.
Left breast. That would
be Lucinda. The one
with the sweetest temperament.

I tried to imagine
the doctor's deliberate
thrust. The giving up
of something Lucinda
had made, perhaps
not as successfully
as milk for the suckling
mouths, but nonetheless
made herself, in the best way
she knew how, trying
to repair whatever it was
that injured her—parting
with that because
of what it means that
the calcium is new.

The radiologist was smiling
the kind of patient smile
she has perfected
talking to women
about the most important
event of their lives.
                I know,

I said, my wife will want
this resolved. Watching
it, is not her style.

And I felt the clicks
of the next steps clacking in
like arrival times
at Grand Central Station—
the biopsy, the pathologist's
cold eye, the favorite surgeon—
and I tried to imagine
what it would be like for her
without Lucinda.
It would be necessary, I concluded,
to give all the more attention
to Lucille.

Thank you, I said to the radiologist, realizing I was thanking her
if not for the news,
for the clarity
of news, which is,
after all the best
one can get. And
I gathered the little images
of her radial rivers
and streams, the understructure
of the beauty I had admired
and named,
gathered them under
my arm.

And I may even
have clutched them
to my breast
as I made the telephone call.

John L. Wright

Bedside Rounds

I thought of bedside rounds
when my landscape architect called to ask
if it was okay to bring an intern with her.
Of course, I say,
remembering the many years I enjoyed teaching
and the few times the house staff
honored me
with the Best Teacher award.

So today she's here to help me reshape
the back lawn to support,
structurally and aesthetically,
a new bluestone walk, its slow curve
leading to a new red cedar porch.
For sure,
this is not a matter of life or death
but after an hour
of traipsing around with her yellow tape
and spray can of orange, water-soluble paint,
asking the intern what she thinks of this border
or that elevation
I begin to resent them
—the little games they play.
Whose lawn
do they think they're talking over
anyway?

The Portugal Laurel

At times I fear,
after decades of doctoring,
of stashing tears in the pockets
of a long white coat,
my soul has turned to salt.
Take, for example, the Portugal Laurel.
It has graced the patio for thirty-five years,
grown up with the family, seen sorrows, joys.
It has provided shade and beauty,
following a morning rain it sparkles
in the afternoon sun, a million pieces
of dark green crystal, carnelian stems.
And many a midnight its branches
have hid the ashes of a sleepless cigar.
But now, children gone, the patio is a ruin.
The landscape architect proclaims,
We need to open this space.
So yesterday I took the laurel down,
not the slightest hesitation. At the start
I was occupied by technical matters—how to
bring down a robust laurel safely,
how to dispose of it. Never mind the details,
but you know I had to use a chain saw—
the trunk was twelve inches at the base.
In an hour and a half it was gone, all except
the weeping stump.
Only then—only when confronted
by that personal void—
did I feel a single shiver of sadness.
See what I mean?
And today? Well, today
I have this pale blue numbness
which I know by tomorrow
will be gone.

※ *Jack Coulehan*

Thirst

On waking, my dry tongue sticks to the top
of my mouth, and I imagine the boy
from Guyana, whose heart wouldn't come back
after the surgeon unscrambled it.
Dried up by drugs and liquid restriction,
the boy is obsessed with Pepsi and juice.
He creeps to his hospital sink at night
when no one is looking; he sits by the door
of his room, like a beggar from Delhi,
whispering, Water, please give me water . . .

I never figured why his heart had failed,
but believed it would take a bad turn.
And soon—either to drown in his own brine
or suffer a death of delirious thirst,
too young to be conned that pulling all stops
to stay alive might be redemptive.
Let the boy die in peace, his mother asked,
if his heart's no good. I stopped the drugs
and wrote for a cover of morphine.

My tongue sticks to the top of my mouth
in the morning. I sleep with mouth open,
much like my father did, when he became old
and infirm, a kind of mummification
that occurs first in sleep, a line in the sand
beyond which it's impossible to predict—
take the boy from Guyana, who feasted
for weeks after we allowed him to die.
He perked up and went home. His heart awoke
from its long sleep and began to pump.

Long Sentence

If you had told me twenty years ago,
that I would attend a meeting
at St. Petersburg Beach
for the tax deduction on Acquired
Immune Deficiency Syndrome, that I
would arrive an hour late because
of a pick-up racquetball game
with Derek, a quick thirty-five-year-old Scot,
and that, having napped through lunch
and smoked a small cigar beneath
a hooded lounge chair for two,
on the beach chatting with you, that
I would pass up a half day of meetings
to sit here at poolside watching couples
watch their children as we did ours
at the O Club pool when we lived down here
twenty-five years ago, I would not
have believed you, but
it's true as the glacier
that never nearly got this far
except in the heart of God who
makes me fear that hemiparetic
who kicks at the ladder of the pool,
and the growing old that strolls up
the beach and down the six lane road.

Bonnie Salomon

Your Last Patient

The day will come, as surely as it started
when the whirlwind of the hospital threw you
into the laps of unsuspecting patients.

Learning under terror, grabbing onto hope
you wouldn't harm the incarcerated patient.
Watching your effortless elders, who seemed
all-knowing
to an unknowing student, shoulders stooped
from heavy booklets filling lab coat pockets.
Like ducklings trailing Momma, you followed
Attending, Resident, Intern, til at last you
led the white coat parade. Momma stops here.

You'll unwrap your final patient,
saved for the party's end
(when all the guests are anxious to leave).
At day's close, signatures and handshakes
signal completion of the task, yet

somewhere the thousand lives you touched
live, maybe thrive, wave goodbye, turning
their backs on your dazzled face
as you whisper, Thank you.

Auscultation

Beyond the stacks
of textbooks studied

among the piles of journals
read and not

pulsing in those
glove-numbed hands

inside the stiff white coat
starched to armor

noosed in the caduceus
drumming deep within

the black coils

between the endless rounds
the endless dyings

still beats
a poet's heart

and it pounds again
and pounds again

now that you have
finally clutched

this instrument
to your own chest.

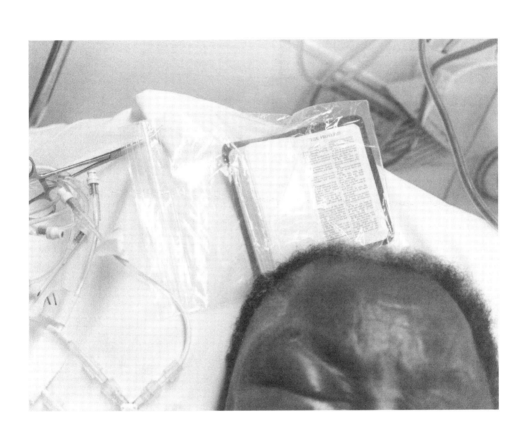

Afterword

About twelve years ago, I had the honor of touring the house in which Dr. William Carlos Williams lived and practiced. The tour was led by Dr. William Eric Williams, the poet's son (and a practicing pediatrician). At one point, William Eric pointed out a small room in which his famous father used to type poems late into the night. I felt privileged to walk into that room and said so. Dr. Williams shot back, "It's just a plain old office." To which I replied, "But surely some of your Dad's atoms are still around this place!" Dr. Williams responded, "I expect so. He did tend to sneeze vigorously."

Certainly, Dr. Williams' atoms are all over and around contemporary poetry today, including the work collected in this unique volume. Williams' influence has been felt by American poets for at least three-quarters of a century, with remarkable effect. James Dickey may have said it best: "Has any other poet in American history been so *actually* useful, usable, and influential?"

I like the derivation of the word "poet." It comes from the Greek, *poiein*, which means "to make." (I also like the shared etymology of "poet" with a medical word like *hematopoiesis*, the "making of blood.") A poet is a maker, then—and the poet's raw materials are words, of course. I've known, through the years, health care professionals who have been artists: fiction writers, biographers, essayists, composers, painters, sculptors, musicians of all sorts, from cellists to clarinetists to gamelan players. But of those who choose to write, a great many choose to write poetry. I believe there are many good reasons for such a choice, including the following:

Poetry tends to be short (Dr. Williams often wrote on a prescription pad, which may have played a physical role in the short lines he often preferred). Poetry can fit into the white coat and be retrieved when time affords. It is there when we need it. In an emergency, poetry can even be written on the white coat itself.

Poetry is portable—it is *the* art form that is easily memorized and carried along into the daily bustle and discombobulation of our lives.

Poetry revels in ambiguity, as does the world. Patients come to clinicians with at least two degrees of ambiguity: ambiguous and more ambiguous. The patient—and his tests—routinely mean more than one thing. Poetry can help us expect, understand, and deal with such ambiguities as they find us. Some in medicine find ambiguity discomfiting; poets recognize it for what it is—and make poems out of it.

Poetry is epigrammatic. It makes us take a deep breath and hold it. It distills the world.

Poetry is epiphanic. An epiphany is the psychic jolt of insight that arises from an apparently mundane encounter, such as those Dr. Williams records: that red wheelbarrow beside the white chickens. Those plums in the icebox. Those broken pieces of a green bottle in the hospital parking lot. Such epiphanies delight, surprise, and renew us in our daily work. They tweak our sense of humor. They make poets reach for something to write on.

Poets know that the Muse doesn't always come when we call her. She can be, by turns, mercurial, stubborn or obstreperous, soft-spoken, smiling, even seductive. At times all we can do is wait for her to come to us. But if we keep our antennae up at just the right height, we can sense when she is there on our shoulders, whispering in our ears. At that point, the best advice is to listen closely—as the poets here have done so well.

—John Stone

Acknowledgments

Thanks to the editors of the following publications where some of these poems have previously appeared:

Richard M. Berlin: "Anatomy Lab," "Inside Out," "January Thaw," and "Learning the Shapes" are reprinted from *How JFK Killed My Father* by Richard M. Berlin (Pearl Editions, 2004). Used by permission of the publisher. "First Night On Call, Coronary Care Unit" appeared in *Psychiatric Times*, April 2003, and is reprinted by permission of the author.

Bryan Maxwell: "Still Life in Number Seven" appeared in *Bellevue Literary Review, Spring 2005, Vol 4 (2)*, and is reprinted by permission of the author. "Light from Dark" appeared in *The Eleventh Muse*, 2004, Vol 44, and is reprinted by permission of the author.

Allen Peterkin: "First Suture" appeared in *Canadian Medical Association Journal*, 2001, Vol 164 (12), and is reprinted by permission of the author.

Sachin B. Patel: "Call Room" appeared in *Minnesota Medicine*, July 2004, Vol 87. Copyright © Sachin B. Patel 2004. Reprinted by permission of *Minnesota Medicine*.

Jerald Winakur: "Auscultation" appeared in *Annals of Internal Medicine*, June 7, 2005, Vol 142 (11). Copyright © Jerald Winakur 2005. Reprinted by permission of *Annals of Internal Medicine*.

John Wright: "Bedside Rounds" appeared in *Journal of the American Medical Association*, 2000, Vol 283 (14). Copyright © John Wright 2000. Reprinted by permission of the Journal of the American Medical Association. "The Portugal Laurel" appeared in *Journal of the American Medical Association*, 1996, Vol 275 (16). Copyright © John Wright 1996. Reprinted by permission of *Journal of the American Medical Association*.

The editors wish to acknowledge the Division of Medical Humanities at the University of Rochester School of Medicine for its initial and ongoing support for this book. We are especially grateful to Jack Coulehan for his editorial intelligence and humor and hours spent reading the manuscript.

And, above all, we would like to thank our patients.

Contributors Notes

Mona Arif was an undergrad at Cornell, graduated from the University of Rochester School of Medicine. She is a pediatrics resident at the University of Texas Southwestern Medical Center.

Richard M. Berlin is a physician whose poetry appears monthly in *Psychiatric Times*. He is the author of *How JFK Killed My Father* which won the Pearl Poetry Prize.

Gregg Chesney is a medical student at the University of Rochester. He hopes to take some time off to earn an MFA, but for now he's much too worried about studying for his Step 1 Boards.

Catharine Clark-Sayles practices internal medicine and geriatrics in California. She stopped writing when she first became a doctor, but rediscovered her passion at age forty.

Sarah Jane Cook is a Maritime Canadian, born and raised in Truro, Nova Scotia. She is a graduate of Dalhousie Medical School and is currently a family medicine residency.

Dagan Coppock attended medical school at Yale and is presently a resident at Beth Israel in Boston, but his heart will always belong to his home state of Tennessee.

Jack Coulehan teaches at Stony Brook University and has two amazing grandchildren. He has recently edited *Second Opinion: Poems by Physicians*.

Michael Doo is currently in training in the Internal Medicine residency program at the University of California-Irvine.

Rishi Doshi is a fourth-year medical student at the University of California at San Diego. He is a poetry editor for his school's arts and literature magazine, *The Human Condition*.

Danny Duke was a member of the Associate Faculty for the Center for Medical Humanities at the University of Texas, San Antonio. He passed away in July 2004.

Frank Edwards has been an emergency physician for 25 years. He's conducted creative writing workshops for medical students in Rochester for a dozen years.

Robert Felix is an avid motorcyclist, climber, and coffee drinker. He graduated from Drexel School of Medicine.

Katherine Freeman, a student at Northeastern Ohio Universities College of Medicine, is still laughing at the obvious, writing about the obscure, and looking out for zebras.

Therese Garrett is a graduate of the University of California-San Francisco School of Medicine. She is a psychiatry resident at Harward Longwood Hospital.

Alberto Hazan was born in Caracas, Venezuela, and moved to the United States when he was nine years old. He is currently in the midst of his Emergency Medicine residency.

Michael Jacobs was born in Santa Monica, California. He was an English major at Pomona College. He is a neurology resident at the University of California-Irvine.

Neeta Jain completed her undergraduate degree at Stanford University and medical school at the University of Rochester. She is an internal medicine resident at California Pacific Medical Center.

Meghann Kaiser is a Family Practitioner in California, where she lives with her husband, Nathan, and all her pets. She is a graduate of the University of California-Irvine School of Medicine.

Ken Kao is a graduate of the University of Rochester School of Medicine. He is currently a general surgery intern at Harbor-UCLA Medical Center.

Mairi Leining graduated from Georgetown University School of Medicine. She is currently an internal medicine resident at Beth Israel Deaconess Medical Center in Boston.

Joel J. Mathew is a medical student at the University at Buffalo, School of Medicine and Biomedical Sciences (SUNY).

Bryan Maxwell grew up in North Carolina and Virginia but now lives in California, where he is a third-year MD/MPH student.

Emilie Osborn is a family physician who has taught medical students, nurses, and residents. She was Associate Dean for Student and Curricular Affairs at the University of California-San Francisco.

Sachin B. Patel graduated from Carleton College with a BA in English. During medical school he developed as a spoken word poet. He is now a medicine resident at the University of North Carolina.

Allan Peterkin is a psychiatrist at the University of Toronto and the author of six books on medicine and cultural history. He is a founding editor of the journal *ARS MEDICA*.

Troy Pittman is a third-year medical student at the University at Buffalo School of Medicine and Biomedical Sciences.

Noah Raizman is a fourth-year medical student and also an MFA candidate in Writing at Columbia University, planning on pursuing a career in Orthopedic Surgery.

Maureen Rappaport is a family physician on faculty at McGill University. She loves to read and write with students, residents, and other healthcare professionals.

Anna Reisman is a general internist and teacher at Yale and Veterans Administration (VA) Connecticut. She coordinates a creative writing program for Yale internal medicine residents.

Renee Rossi is an otolaryngologist on the faculty at University of Texas Southwestern. She is currently working on an MFA in Creative Writing (poetry) at Vermont College.

Bonnie Salomon is an emergency physician in the Chicago area. She teaches medical ethics in the Philosophy Department of Lake Forest College.

Beth Seltzer is a writer and former filmmaker who still wonders sometimes how she ended up with an MD. As a resident she wonders how to translate her poetry into a life of medicine.

Audrey Shafer is an associate professor of anesthesia at Stanford University School of Medicine. She has written a children's novel due to be published by Random House.

Mindy Shah studied English at Colgate University, after which she trained in medicine at the University of Rochester. She is currently a fellow in geriatrics.

Stephanie Snow trained at Dalhousie medical school in Halifax, Nova Scotia, and is presently an internal medicine resident there.

Parker Towle has been a neurologist in New Hampshire for forty-two years. He teaches at Dartmouth Medical School and is Associate Editor at *The Worcester Review.*

Emily R. Transue is a general internist in Seattle and the author of *On Call: A Doctor's Days and Nights in Residency.*

Stephen Vadenhoff received a bachelor's in English Literature from the University of Virginia. He is currently a medical student at Drexel University College of Medicine.

David Watts grew up in Central Texas and trained first as a musician then as a medical doctor. His practice of medicine and gastroenterology is at the University of California-San Francisco.

Kelley Jean White has been a pediatrician in inner-city Philadelphia for twenty-five years. A book of her "medical" poetry was recently published by The People's Press.

Karen Wilson is a pediatrics resident at the University of Rochester. She spends what little free time she has with her (very patient) husband Cole and their two children.

Jerald Winakur has been at the practice of internal and geriatric medicine for thirty years. He lives in the Texas hill country where he watches birds and raises native plants.

John L. Wright is a seventy-five-year-old retired internist and endocrinologist who wrote his first poem in 1988.

Sue Sun Yom graduated from the University of Pennsylvania with an MD/PhD in literature. She is currently a radiation oncology resident in Houston, Texas.

John Yowpa III is a graduate of Cornell University and Upstate Medical University and is currently a medicine/pediatrics resident at the University at Buffalo.

About the Editors

Neeta Jain grew up in Las Vegas, Nevada. After completing her undergraduate degree at Stanford University and medical school at the University of Rochester, she returned to the west coast for internal medicine residency training at California Pacific Medical Center in San Francisco. Her interests include medical humanities, public health, and being a good doctor.

Dagan Coppock was born in Knoxville, Tennessee. He received his BS in biology from the University of Tennessee. Following his undergraduate training, he lived in Nigeria as a Fulbright scholar where he researched the poetry of traditional healers. He graduated from Yale School of Medicine and is currently a medical resident at Beth Israel Deaconess Medical Center in Boston.

Stephanie Brown Clark is a Canadian with an MA in English Literature from the University of Western Ontario and an MD from McMaster University. She completed her PhD in medical history and English literature at the University of Leiden in the Netherlands in 1998 and is currently an Assistant Professor in the Division of Medical Humanities at the University of Rochester Medical Center where she teaches medical history, literature, and medicine and helps with creative student projects like this one.

BOA Anthology Series

✻